ESCAPING THE HAMSTI

A Disruptive Approach to
Solutioning Complex Business Problems

Ida P. Mack

LUMIN ESSENCE
CONSULTING GROUP

Published in the United States by

LuminEssence Consulting Group LLC.

ISBN: 979-8-9903135-0-7 (Print)

ISBN: 979-8-9903135-1-4 (E-Book)

Library of Congress Control Number: 2024910333

First printing edition 2024

Escape the Hamster Wheel™

38045 47th St. East #102

Palmdale, CA 93552

www.idapmack.com

To Pato and Kawan

ESCAPING THE HAMSTER WHEEL

CONTENTS

PART THREE

Disrupt with Purpose

❀ ❀ ❀

ESCAPING THE HAMSTER WHEEL

INTRODUCTION

I.

Escaping the Hamster Wheel: A Disruptive Approach to Solutioning Complex Business Problems stems from my passion for problem solutioning and the sheer frustration I've felt over the years watching various initiatives struggle to solution the very problems they were designed to address. Like many of you, I've navigated the challenging landscape of these intricate issues, often experiencing the good, the bad, and the downright ugly of complex problem solutioning.

While my success in solutioning complex business problems has varied over the years, the outcomes were rarely attributed solely to the execution of the initiative itself. They were influenced by several factors, including the level of leadership support, staff commitment, degree of politics, impact on an organization's general and sub-cultures, and ability to adapt and accept change. I've weathered frustrations stemming from my leaders' strategic decisions to their prioritization of politics and personal agendas over leveraging industry best practices. I've also observed scenarios where colleagues, despite their best intentions, lacked the necessary skills for complex business problem solutioning, which highlighted systematic challenges within an organization. At times, despite my genuine desire to help, I've been sidelined. This was either because my vision did not align with leadership, other agendas took precedence, or there was simply a lack of interest in learning about a new or unfamiliar approach.

Climbing the corporate ladder has never been my aspiration. Shockingly, I have never had a five-year plan, let alone a 10-year plan, for my career trajectory. Instead, I've always sought out roles that I believed would challenge me and provide opportunities to develop new skills aligned with my passions: process improvement and problem solutioning. This career strategy has been pivotal in building a reputation to be able to solution the unsolvable. Early in my career, I committed to mastering the art of process improvement, and I knew this would be a lifelong journey. As I worked towards mastering various disciplines, I recognized what I perceived to be an unspoken crisis across industries: the consistent inability to prevent and, subsequently, successfully solution complex business problems. I recognized a need to disrupt modern-day problem solutioning and created the TAAP™ approach.

From employee resistance to a lack of leadership accountability, many factors contribute to the staggering 70% failure rate of change initiatives in the U.S., as reported by Forbes. This percentage does not consider initiatives that fall outside of this category, yet it underscores the urgent need for disruption. Interestingly, this statistic can be traced to an assertion made by John Kotter, who is known for his work in leadership development and change management over 25 years ago! It is accepted as the benchmark or industry standard when looking at the success of change initiatives and business transformations. The critical question is whether the number remains valid 25 years after its original assertion. Nevertheless, overcoming the odds to address complex business problems in your organization is not hopeless; it is possible with the right approach.

Before progressing further, you must understand the difference between a framework, methodology, and approach. Although often used interchangeably, each has a distinct meaning and purpose.

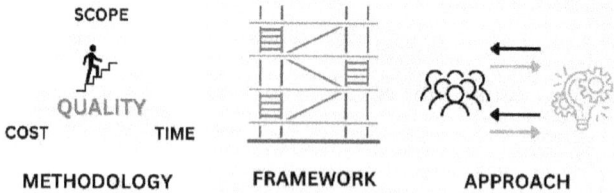

SCOPE

QUALITY

COST   TIME

METHODOLOGY   **FRAMEWORK**   **APPROACH**

A **framework** acts as a conceptual backbone, offering guidelines and principles to understand complex issues and problems when organizing information. It is the big-picture view outlining key components and their interconnections. Like scaffolding, a framework provides a structure with multiple pathways to navigate solutioning to complex business problems, allowing for flexibility and the ability to pivot quickly when faced with change. A **methodology** is comprised of a set of practices, techniques, or rules tailored to achieve a specific goal or outcome. It's like a road map guiding you through set-by-step processes and best practices. Methodologies are rigid in structure and may not be ideal when solutioning complex business problems because they can stifle creativity and innovation by imposing strict constraints. The **approach** is broader in scope. It embodies your overall strategy or mindset when facing complex problem business problems head-on. It sets the course for your actions and is ideal when solutioning complex business problems because it encourages flexibility, creativity, and adaptability. Unlike rigid methodologies, an approach allows for nuanced problem solutioning explicitly tailored for the unique challenges of each business situation, promoting innovation when faced with uncertainty.

Understanding the distinction between a framework, methodology, and approach is crucial as you navigate your leadership journey. It is worth noting that Agile differs from methodologies. **Agile** is a framework, and its practitioners adopt principles without adhering to specific methods, emphasizing flexibility in complex business problem solutioning. This understanding underscores the notion that you don't "do" Agile but embody its principles. You *are* Agile. This shift in perspective fosters a culture of continuous improvement, innovation, and sustainability, empowering leaders to thrive in dynamic environments.

While leaders may have the frameworks and methodologies to tackle complex business problems, the question remains: Do leaders have the mindset necessary to execute effective problem-solutioning? I've witnessed senior-level leaders make decisions based on unvalidated assumptions while neglecting to conduct feasibility and impact assessments, which are crucial to gauge the realism of their planned approach, estimated timeframes, and resource allocations. Consequently, they overlook their decisions' broader short- and long-term impacts on the organization and its employees.

Although collaborating in teams is essential, the challenges a team faces are far too significant to achieve the desired impact by the time a leader forms a team. Not to mention, the persistent pressure from leadership to rush solutions only exacerbates the situation. It highlights the crucial need for a disruptive approach that prioritizes mindset, adaptability, and accountability over mere planning. This balance is vital for fostering long-term success and guarding against short-sighted demands of individuals or groups in positions of authority.

I will never understand why leadership incessantly pushes for a rush to solutions, even when it is clear that doing so will jeopardize sustainable value-added success. In my experience, this behavior appears to stem from decision-making rooted in an underlying fear of consequences such as backlash, political influences, a desperate need for survival or self-preservation, or the pursuit of power within the organization. Unfortunately, when these dynamics are at play, the opportunity for successful complex business problem solutioning significantly diminishes, sometimes to almost none. I find this both frustrating and heartbreaking to witness.

Over time, I came to understand the crux of the issue didn't lie within the execution of the frameworks or methodologies themselves but rather within the leaders tasked with their selection and strategy for execution. There is a common thread among these individuals - a thread woven from their mindset to their ability to align with the company's culture and withstand conformity and political pressures. At the same time, they must be capable of purposefully disrupting and driving innovation to stay ahead of changes in market and technological advancements. This resilience I've found dictates their success in executing initiatives to solve complex business problems. Leaders must recognize that with every change, innovation, and introduction of a new competitor to the market, complex business problems increase in complexity while decreasing the likelihood of successful solutioning. There must be a balance. This common thread must occur well before a framework or methodology is selected; it is a thread that should be woven into the very essence of the organization's culture and owned by each leader.

Solutioning complex business problems isn't typically integrated into day-to-day operations. Problems of this magnitude don't manifest overnight; they simmer and evolve gradually over time. They are often treated as temporary hurdles rather than long-term strategic imperatives. Once I realized this, I felt compelled to act. I couldn't simply continue to observe passively as more initiatives failed. I am sure that, as leaders, we have shared experiences that transcend industry boundaries. Irrespective of the sector, leadership style, or methodology, there are a few common denominators as to why efforts to solution complex business problems remain pervasive:

1. The effort did not follow a disciplined framework or methodology.
2. The wrong framework or methodology was selected.
3. The chosen framework or methodology was not implemented correctly.

This led me to question why.

Why do 70% of change initiatives fail? Why hasn't anyone systematically collected data on the initiatives outside this category? Why is leadership development primarily focused on empowering trainers and coaches to teach theories and problem-solving tools to leaders? Why isn't there a greater emphasis on the expectations of leaders for self-empowerment and internal skill development? Why is there often a lack of accountability for leaders responsible for building systems and driving organizational culture? And why do initiatives continue to struggle despite the abundance of mature, industry-recognized frameworks and methodologies?

We can take specific actions to confront these challenges head-on and improve the success rate of initiatives aimed at solutioning complex business problems. By addressing these questions, we can pave the way for tangible improvements.

Before we move any further, let me clarify something. You may have read the word "solutioning" and thought, *what in the world is she saying?!* Well, throughout this book, I use **solution** instead of **solve**. My intent behind this is to highlight the difference between the *process* and the *final product,* namely showing when you solve something, it indicates the end, which suggests you are done. But we aren't done when we are *solutioning.* We are actively looking for answers and working on implementing solutions to not only achieve the outcome we want but to continuously sustain the results we've put in place while keeping a pulse on the market to transform, align, adapt, and pivot when necessary.

II.

Allow me to introduce the approach - a disruptive approach that harnesses the power of agility to solution complex business problems. What makes TAAP™ disruptive? It focuses on metacognition and self-empowerment, which involves leaders taking ownership and developing awareness and control over their cognitive processes. The strategic application of metacognition empowers leaders to cultivate the adaptive mindset necessary for effectively navigating and solutioning complex business problems. By fostering self-awareness, self-accountability, reflective thinking, and proactive strategies, metacognition equips leaders with the cognitive agility and resilience required to lead the charge toward successful problem solutioning.

TAAP™ is an agile approach; it is flexible, adaptable, and designed to place ownness on the leader before a framework or methodology is selected to:

T ransform a leader's mindset to embrace a Transformative Agile™ leadership style.

A lign a leader's personal values and ethics with those of their organization to lead with integrity.

A dapt and embrace Disruptive Problem Solutioning™.

P ivot at any time to ensure a leader's mindset and approach align with the ever-changing and ever-evolving business and technological landscapes.

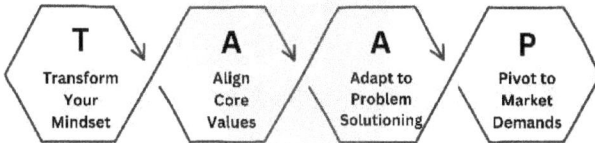

T	**A**	**A**	**P**
Transform Your Mindset	Align Core Values	Adapt to Problem Solutioning	Pivot to Market Demands

PURPOSE

I.

I was blessed with opportunities to work across multiple industries and disciplines (e.g., social services, healthcare, entertainment, finance, etc.) while learning how to successfully solution complex business problems; I have had opportunities to lead teams while building relationships with colleagues who have a similar passion and skill set. From working with operations staff whose level of thinking outside-the-box will make you want to create problems simply to watch them develop creative solutions, to the systematic approach of technology staff who produce a synchronized cadence to problem solutioning that is inexplicably adaptable and rooted in industry and Agile best practices, I've done it all. (Well, mostly). My technology colleagues introduced me to Lean Six Sigma and Agile, and this is where I began my journey to identify how to transition these disciplines to operations!

I recognized that leveraging the Lean Six Sigma Methodology - a systematic approach that aims to reduce waste and improve efficiencies and Agile, which focuses on collaboration, flexibility, and responsiveness to change, could elevate my process improvement and complex business problem solutioning skills. This was the first time I realized I could get far more benefits from leveraging more than one approach or methodology while attempting to improve processes. I also understood that there is a dark side when a business does not use the proper tools to solution complex business problems. Uninformed and rash decisions coupled with a lack of leadership support can have far-reaching effects on an organization and its employees. After witnessing entire departments be dissolved, the leaders who contributed to or allowed the problem to fester were left unscathed. However, they were ultimately responsible but failed to develop a successful strategy to solution the problem. These leaders were rewarded. They were allowed to have a do-over at the previous employees' expense. Their jobs remained intact. Where is the accountability?

Given my lack of interest in climbing the corporate ladder and engaging in professional political warfare, I needed a broader platform to share my approach to solutioning complex business problems in hopes of helping to end this cycle. My intent is not to place blame, critique, or judge any leader but to provide a resource to help you excel in your role. This book is the first step in reaching a broader audience.

II.

In *Escaping the Hamster Wheel*, my mission is clear empower leaders to transform their mindset and approach to solution complex business problems. Through the TAAP™ approach, you will develop a deep understanding of who you are at your core. By way of metacognition, you can **empower yourself** to transform your mindset and dissect what you need to become a leader who defies the status quo and leads your organization and team to solution complex business problems successfully!

This book is more than just a collection of theories, methodologies, and case studies; it is a roadmap for action and a blueprint for transformation. I share with you my professional experiences and challenge you to do the work to become a leader skilled in Transformative Agile™ so that you can influence organizational culture to drive meaningful change while empowering yourself at the same time.

From cultivating an agile mindset, to discerning the difference between a complex business problem and a symptom of a complex business problem, to fostering a culture of continuous improvement to sustain the integrity of your solutions while being purposefully disruptive, you will leave no stone unturned in your quest for *excellence*.

III.

As you proceed, you will actively gain insight into what is necessary to transform into a leader adept at navigating purposeful disruption. The journey towards leadership transformation will be both challenging and rewarding. It is about internal growth and self-empowerment. It is a path that must be traversed alone.

While the journey must be undertaken alone, *Escaping the Hamster Wheel Workbook* is a valuable companion, offering metacognitive exercises designed to guide and support you as you embark on your path to TAAP™ for self-empowerment and leadership development. The workbook guides your understanding of key concepts and cultivates the resilience and adaptability needed to confront challenges head-on. Embrace this opportunity to maximize your learning experience and utilize the workbook to its fullest extent.

PART ONE

Lead with Integrity

ETHICAL LEADERSHIP AND ORGANIZATIONAL CULTURE

I.

Whether you are asked to lead a group, be a subject matter expert on a topic, or speak up briefly and facilitate a group discussion, most of us will take on a leadership role at some point in our lives. While everyone should understand what type of leader they are, I am explicitly referencing those who have or are striving towards a career in leadership. Before we proceed, it is crucial to establish a shared understanding of what the terms 'leader' and 'leadership' mean. Assuming we operate from a uniform definition can be misleading, as interpretations vary widely. For example, for some, leadership may entail simply being in charge and issuing commands. For others, it may involve guiding and influencing a team towards shared objectives with clear accountability for outcomes. Recognizing this spectrum of perspectives lays a solid foundation as you embark on your journey to escape the hamster wheel.

For alignment, a **leader** is a professional who may or may not have subordinate staff but is responsible for executing an organization's vision, goal, or core objective. Now that we're on the same page about what defines a leader let's align with our understanding of 'leadership.' **Leadership** encompasses the collective qualities and behaviors exhibited by a leader. It's not just about holding a title or occupying a position of authority; it's about the actions, behaviors, and decisions that a leader demonstrates in their role. Leadership is the tangible outcome of a leader's efforts to inspire, motivate, and achieve an assigned vision by defining objectives and guiding their team toward success.

You may wonder, "Why is she taking me through definitions I already know?" As someone who has worked with highly competent and capable leaders, I learned not to take clear communication for granted long ago. If we are not clear and aligned upfront on critical terms, we could be interpreting different things. Let's delve into a real-world example that underscores the importance of this principle.

CASE STUDY 1

Interpreting Shared Language

During my tenure as a consultant in the entertainment industry, I led a large process improvement initiative spanning three major divisions with global offices. The project held promise—a chance to revolutionize operations and drive efficiency across the board. After a promising meeting with senior leadership where enthusiasm ran high, and action items were agreed upon, I felt a surge of optimism. The collaboration seemed seamless, and I relished the opportunity to work with such a motivated team. However, my optimism was soon met with a surprising realization during a routine check-in. One of the directors, who had been a vocal advocate for the initiative, had failed to submit her work. Puzzled, I investigated further, only to uncover a tangled web of miscommunication. It turned out that terminology and processes were used interchangeably across divisions, leading to confusion and inefficiency. Adding to the confusion, we learned a system bore the same name as one of the organization's processes. Rather than dwelling on the mistake, we sprang into action. Collaboratively, we devised a solution: a Terms and Definitions book detailing the nuances of terminology and processes across divisions. The director, eager to make amends, volunteered to spearhead the project. This journey to clarity revealed the importance of language alignment to ensure effective communication and collaboration.

In a world where language shapes understanding and action, clarity is paramount. Case Study 1 underscores the need for leaders to take proactive measures to bridge communication gaps and foster alignment from the beginning of any engagement. By addressing issues head-on and embracing a spirit of collaboration, you can pave the way for success and innovation in even the most complex of endeavors. This is only one example; I've encountered numerous miscommunications that have shaped my approach. As a result, I've developed a practice of reaffirming outcomes and actions before, during, and after all team meetings. I've worked with teams to compile a live list of key terms and definitions for larger cross-functional groups to ensure alignment.

❀ ❀ ❀

II.

Ethical leaders lead with integrity; they possess a deep understanding of their values and boundaries. They navigate challenges with resilience and stand firm in their convictions. When faced with adversity, they do not falter. Instead, they draw from their unwavering commitment to do what is right. If confronted with a decision that could compromise their integrity, ethical leaders choose the path that aligns with their principles, even if it means facing opposition and difficulty. In some instances, this could mean imprisonment or death. This dedication to ethical conduct inspires trust and respect among their colleagues, subordinates, and, in some cases, the world.

Would You Be Willing to Die for Your Ethical Beliefs? What were you doing at the age of 21? In 1943, Sophie Scholl, a 21-year-old German student, was arrested with her brother Hans and a fellow student named Christopher Probst. They were caught by the Gestapo distributing leaflets opposing the Nazi regime's atrocities and urging German citizens to resist policies of oppression and genocide. They were interrogated, tried, and sentenced to death by guillotine. What makes Sophie an ethical leader? It was not simply because she was brave and spoke up like her brother and classmate. It was because she was reportedly courageous during the trial despite the risks to her life. She did not beg for mercy or renounce her ethical values in hopes of being spared. Instead, Sophie defended her actions with integrity. Eighty years later, Sophie, Hans, and Christopher remain symbols of resistance against oppression and champions of human rights. Sophie is a model for many who strive to be an ethical leader.

Could You Persevere if You Were Physically Attacked and Your Life Threatened? Does the name Fannie Lou Hamer mean anything to you? Fannie Lou Hamer, a civil rights activist in Mississippi, played a prominent role in securing voting rights for Black people in America. In 1963,

Ms. Hamer and a group of fellow activists attended a voter registration workshop. On their way home, the group was arrested by local law enforcement and jailed. They were brutally beaten and denied medical attention. Once released, Ms. Hamer did not waiver. She co-founded the *Mississippi Freedom Democratic Party* and challenged the all-white Mississippi delegation at the 1964 Democratic National Convention. Her testimony shone a light on the injustices faced by Black voters in Mississippi. It also brought national attention to the issue of voting rights and helped to galvanize support for the civil rights movement. Fannie Lou Hamer's legacy continues to inspire activists fighting for civil rights and social justice today.

Could You Take on Major Corporations to Shine a Light on What's Right? In a world where corporations prioritize profit over ethical considerations, where animal experimentation is the norm, and ethical sourcing and community engagement are insignificant, Anita Roddick was ahead of her time. Anita Roddick founded *The Body Shop* in 1976 and revolutionized the cosmetic industry by prioritizing ethical sourcing, cruelty-free products, and community empowerment. She went against the grain and created her own path. She challenged conventional business models and created a new model whose foundation was rooted in ethical behaviors. She championed causes such as fair trade, animal rights, and environmental conservation. However, she faced many challenges, including having to meet regulatory requirements designed for animal testing without testing on animals. Mrs. Roddick never wavered, and 48 years later, *The Body Shop* is still a global cosmetic organization known for its ethical business model, which many other organizations in the cosmetics industry have adopted.

Would You Prioritize Peace over Revenge? When I think of notable ethical leaders, I think of Nelson Mandela, who spent 27 years in prison for his attempts to overthrow the apartheid regime in South Africa. What makes Nelson Mandela an ethical leader? In 1990, when he was released from prison and subsequently elected president of South Africa, he maintained his principles built on justice, equality, and reconciliation. He prioritized his principles over seeking revenge despite enduring personal suffering for over two decades. If Mr. Mandela had sought justice or revenge, it would have more than likely resulted in widespread violence with countless deaths. Can you imagine? This ethical leader chose the welfare of his people over individual justice! Nelson Mandela remains a timeless example to many leaders today of how to remain ethical in the face of adversity and lead with integrity.

What do Sophie Scholl, Fannie Lou Hamer, Anita Roddick, and Nelson Mandela have in common as ethical leaders? They had a vision, believed in what they were doing, and were unwavering in their course of action. They were clear on their core values, which drove them to remain steadfast regardless of risks as they faced conflicting cultural norms and values.

When we speak of ethical leaders who have achieved what seems to be the impossible, there is a tendency to immortalize them as if they had some superpower or super strength. In reality, they are human like us. I am sure Sophie was afraid to die. I am sure Fannie's pain from being brutally beaten resulted in tears and frustrations that made her want to give up. I am sure Anita experienced unthinkable challenges being a woman in a male-dominated industry. I am sure Nelson's reflection on the years he lost with his family made him feel anger toward his oppressors. Here is the thing: none of this stopped these ethical leaders, as they allowed little to no time for feelings of powerlessness, apathy, anger, frustration, or hopelessness. They recognized these emotions as distractions derailing them from their vision, so they persevered.

III.

If you are questioning the relevance of the historical context provided or struggling to see the connection with your role as a modern-day leader, consider it through the lens of power dynamics. Each of these historical figures challenged the status quo and confronted others with significantly more power, including entire governments. When you solution complex business problems, you will encounter challenges and face the resistance of those wielding more power than you. It is wise to garner the support of senior leadership. However, understand that this can be complicated as your efforts to solution the complex business problem may inadvertently expose weaknesses in processes within departments or challenge decisions made by those higher up in the hierarchy.

Solutioning complex business problems is not easy, especially when many companies in the U.S. have transitioned to a matrixed organization model. McKinsey & Company reports that 84% of employees report working in some extent of a matrixed environment. While designed to streamline the flow of decision-making and communication, a matrixed environment often introduces conflict due to employees engaged in cross-functional work. This leads to dependencies, overlapping hierarchies, and disputes in decision-making processes across the organization. In addition, disputes may also arise due to differing priorities, goals, and perspectives as departments work to meet the strategic objectives of the company. Encouraging people to avoid defensiveness or playing the blame game can be complicated. It requires keeping everyone focused on the collective goal when they have competing priorities.

Furthermore, you may face political, emotional, and personal attacks. From personal experience, I can attest that these attacks can be hurtful and may make you want to give up. However, with time and experience, I've learned that these challenges present opportunities for growth, collaboration, and ultimately triumph. It is about persevering despite the obstacles and finding ways to shape your stepping stones into a path toward success.

IV.

Ethical leaders possess a depth of emotional intelligence (EQ) that serves as a compass guiding them through the complexities of their experiences without deterring them from realizing their vision. These leaders exhibit keen awareness of their emotions and demonstrate the ability to empathize with others. According to research presented in *Emotional EQ 2.0*, two-thirds of the population are controlled by their emotions, yet lack the necessary skills to recognize their own emotions and use them to their advantage.

EQ also plays a pivotal role in your professional success, serving as the single most significant predictor of workplace performance and the primary driver for leadership excellence. As a leader, are you confident in your EQ? If you are uncertain, I strongly recommend you read *Emotional Intelligence 2.0* by Dr. Bradberry and Dr. Greaves. This book offers insights into what EQ entails, practical strategies to enhance your emotional intelligence, and provides the most effective EQ assessment available on the market.

As part of my journey to becoming the leader want to be, I am actively improving my EQ, and I encourage you to embark on a similar journey.

CASE STUDY 2
Emotional Intelligence

While working for a major corporation, I was tasked with solutioning a complex business problem. As I got closer to the final steps of bringing various departments together after spending two years strategically working towards solutioning this problem, I faced a level of resistance I had never experienced in my career. Walking away from this experience, I genuinely understood when my father tried to explain to me what it felt like to be called the "N-word" growing up as a Black boy in the 1940s. There is a feeling of anger, frustration, and powerlessness when a majority group has authority over you. For example, if they accuse you of anything, you would be considered guilty simply because they said so. There is no accountability on their part when they are proven wrong.

I was coincidentally written up seven months after an interaction with a colleague. This occurred right when I was about to bring everyone together to execute the solution. My write-up claimed that multiple colleagues and peers no longer felt comfortable working with me. The claim was not valid. Numerous people from all levels asked when we would start; everyone was looking forward to kicking off the initiative. It was an egregious exaggeration of the actual incident and clearly a microaggression that felt like a *major* aggression to me. I chose to go through Human Resources (HR) to clear my name, and although the language was removed, the insinuation and the weight behind the accusation remained.

What was more hurtful, and honestly psychologically and emotionally traumatic, were the words "verbally accost," which I perceived to have misogynistic, bigoted undertones to it. Of course, it's believable that I, a Black woman, was capable of being aggressive and inciting fear. So much so that my colleagues feared for their physical safety and no longer felt comfortable working with me. I felt like I had been labeled as an *Angry Black Woman* and *Dangerous!* To this day, I am not over this and never will be. Although the language was changed, I asked for an apology in writing and was told "that's not going to happen" by HR. I recognized legally that they could not altogether remove it or apologize because it would be admitting guilt, exposing them to a major lawsuit. The damage was done. It was not worth my reputation or my mental health. This is one of the few times I gave up.

Reflecting on my experience in Case Study 2, my vision remained clear, but I was blind to the barriers in front of me:

1. I formed and trained an Agile team to be self-empowered to solution complex business problems. Unfortunately, the team, which was in place for two years, was immediately dissolved after I received the write up.
2. My leader usurped a workshop I organized for senior leaders to gain buy-in. The day before, my leader had extensive discussions with the senior leaders, resulting in them coming into my workshop with a decision already made. This workshop, approved by my leader, took me a month to design and was canceled during the workshop.

3. I was informed by two decision-making senior leaders, one being my direct leader, that although my proposal to solution the problem would work, they were more concerned with it turning into the "Ida show." This proposal was agile and required collaboration and ownership across all departments within the division. I designed the proposal to empower the senior leaders to own the execution.

Yet, I persevered. However, what stopped me in my tracks was when the organization hit below the belt by removing me as the initiative's lead. I was informed I would be one of five staff considered to lead the effort in the future through an interview process. I was also told that I was valued and that my two years of work would not be in vain but leveraged as they progressed forward. I viewed this as the organization benefiting from my skills and expertise without having to work with me directly. Further adding insult, I sat through a meeting and watched another staff member present my materials in their name without even consulting me.

I realized this was not my problem to solution, and I would instead share my approach with those who will value me and what I have to offer, rather than fight to help those who only see me as a Black woman who should stay in her place. What I failed to realize at the time, if they allowed me - a lower ranking employee, a Black woman - to solution this problem, it would raise questions about their competence and how they allowed this problem to fester for years. Through a process of metacognition, I then understood that this attack on me was rooted in fear and had nothing to do with me as a person, my qualifications, or the relationships - rooted in transparency, honesty, and respect - I'd worked so hard to build with my colleagues.

I share this with you not to gain pity or make myself the victim. I am not a victim, nor will I ever be. My father taught me that I have the power to control how I react and choose how people, places, and things affect me. That said, I refused (and continue to refuse) to allow this experience to make me feel small or deter me from my goals. I chose to take away valuable lessons:

1. Be aware of who is affected when you are implementing change.
2. Be okay with not being as emotionally strong as you believe you are.
3. Be okay with it not being your problem to solution and have the strength to walk away.

This topic is sensitive, but I want to ensure you understand that it will not always be roses and daisies. You will face opposition, and the risks may sometimes be high.

Regardless of your role, I encourage you to be conscious of the impact of the change you are making on others around you. While it could benefit the organization, it could be viewed as a threat. If your efforts affect your emotional and mental health, it is okay to walk away, especially if you do not own the organization. It simply means this is not your problem to solution.

⚇ ⚇ ⚇

As you progress through the book, you must transition your mindset from solely relying on readily available tools to solution complex business problems to enhancing your leadership abilities. This will enable you to cultivate environments conducive to successfully implementing problem-solving tools. It's also important to accept that not every problem is yours to solution; you must know when to persevere and when to step away gracefully.

You will experience your unique challenges and must be mentally prepared to face them. One thing I encourage you to do is know your vulnerabilities and boundaries. It never occurred to me that being a Black woman would be used against me. Not once. I was confronted with my emotional intelligence when racially targeted, which left me vulnerable. I am now keenly aware of the infamous double-negative that Black women have to navigate in America, particularly in the workplace. This convergence of racism and sexism creates unique challenges that are compounded by the easily imposed and accepted stereotypes. I am determined to avoid situations where I feel powerless and where my reputation or character might be unfairly tainted by racial bias.

Suppose you are offended or believe that my experience with discrimination has no place in complex problem solutioning. In that case, I encourage you to think of the people you lead and what inherent biases you may have or have experienced. These biases disadvantaged the organization in Case Study 2, limiting opportunities for creativity and innovation, while also risking the loss of valuable employees. Reflecting on your own experiences and biases through metacognition requires more than surface-level observation; it entails deeply exploring your inherent biases. Instead of mentally outlining or documenting what you experienced or how you behaved, delve deeper and ask yourself why. We all have biases. And at some point, we have experienced bias ourselves. You can become a more effective leader by learning to empathize with the detrimental effects of bias (e.g., discrimination) on individuals and the organization. You'll be capable of forming cross-functional, diverse teams positioned to effectively solution complex business problems.

How often have you sat in a meeting or been a part of a team where everyone was a part of the same cultural or ethnic group? Or the opposite, were you ever the only person of your cultural or ethnic group where there was a majority of a specific group? As an ethical leader who leads with integrity and is committed to a vision and solutioning complex business problems (that was a mouthful!), it is imperative that you have these personal conversations. Know your inherent biases. Know your fears. Know your prejudices. Know your biased assumptions. This is work you need to do for yourself.

I have sat in rooms where I am the lowest ranking and only Black person, and there were no people of color on the team, either. I have also taken part in well-balanced, diverse teams, and I can tell you firsthand that the variety of life experiences and perspectives makes a difference. Please keep this in mind while hiring people and selecting your teams. Solutioning complex business problems goes beyond assembling a group of people you personally feel are intelligent and relatable; it's about uniting people from diverse backgrounds, cultures, and experiences. Through the fusion of perspectives, we unlock an unparalleled level of creativity and innovation. Each unique viewpoint contributes to a collective intelligence transcending what any individual or cultural group could achieve alone.

V.

I vividly remember the first time I took a stand for myself professionally. Looking back, I realize that my motivations may not have aligned entirely with leading with integrity because I was primarily focused on my concerns. However, in retrospect, I recognize that my actions served as an example to other leaders of the importance of advocating for one's beliefs. Despite the initial self-centeredness of my approach, I inadvertently demonstrated the courage to assert myself and paved the way for others to do the same.

CASE STUDY 3

Upholding Ethics & Values Amidst Adversity

Early in my career, I worked as a house leader in an all-male group home for youth aged 13 -21 on probation. I was responsible for approximately 13 staff members and 84 probation youth. This was not a typical job for women. In fact, at the time of this incident, I was the only female leader and worked the overnight shift.

One of the responsibilities of the leader was to distribute cash on the weekends to the youth who were granted a home pass. This was a significant responsibility because, at any given time, we could have over 1000 dollars in the office

34

from Wednesday to Sunday. In addition, there would be extra funds for the youth who would go on facility activities if they weren't granted a home pass. The organization did not provide a physical safe or secure process for tracking or distributing the funds. The money was kept in a metal box without a lock, and anyone with a key to the leaders' office had access to the funds. No leader was allowed on the premises outside of their shift.

I had heard rumors that one of the leaders had a substance abuse problem, and before I was hired, cash in the office often went missing during the night shift. Everyone suspected this individual was stealing the money, but they couldn't prove it. This raised serious issues and exposed the organization to audits from the Department of Probation because, for some youths, the money they were given was all they had for purchasing food while on home pass. The organization was at risk of potentially losing its license to operate.

One weekend, I was on shift, and the day leader informed me that money had been missing from the office the previous week. The executive director sent an email informing all leaders that if cash came up missing again, we would all have to pay for it equally out of our checks, as we were a team. As you can imagine, this did not sit too well with me for a multitude of reasons. Firstly, I am not a thief, and I deplore thieves. Secondly, why would I be held accountable for someone's actions that I have no control over?! Lastly, I should get paid for the hours I worked. I spoke with my father about my concern and his advice was to make sure no one comes on my shift and never to leave the money in the office. He also advised that I place the money in a different location but not carry it on me in case I am accused of attempting to steal it.

Every night when my shift started, I would take the money from the drawer and place it in a heavy locked safe in the spare tire compartment of my car, which also had a lock. I would then set the car alarm in the event someone tried to break into my car. I also parked directly under the security camera in the parking lot to ensure clear video footage in case anything happened. In the morning, I would collect the money, and during the transition with the morning shift leader, I would count the money out loud and have them sign the logbook confirming the amount received, as well as a receipt book for my personal records. This process went on for about a month.

One night, the leader everyone suspected of stealing showed up during my shift. I saw him entering the building near the leaders' office while I was returning from my patrol of the building. I asked him what he was doing in the building, and he said he was just stopping by to say hi to the night staff. I informed him he was not allowed in the building and would have to leave. He laughed and said, "Come on, I am just going to say hi. It's not that serious. I have insomnia and live up the street." I told him that if he did not leave, I would contact the executive director and call the police, as the policy states. I also mentioned the rumors and why I hoped they were false because I respected him. He was not mean or disrespectful; he thanked me for telling him about the rumors. Interestingly, he didn't say he wasn't stealing. He eventually left. I made a note in the logbook about the incident. I found it perplexing that no one else spoke up and said (logged) that he was in the facility after hours on their shift. As you can imagine, the next day, everyone was discussing what I had done. Another month went by, and on another night shift, money came up missing. It was over 1400 dollars! The leader on shift said they believed they saw the leader whom we all suspected was stealing, but they could not confirm that it was him.

During our bi-weekly group supervision meeting on the day shift, the executive director informed us that we would each have money deducted from our next paycheck to make up for the stolen funds. As I sat with this group of men, most with their heads hung low, no one except myself and the person everyone suspected of stealing looked at the executive director. I waited to see if they would say anything. They didn't. They were all great guys - more senior than me - and I loved working with each of them. But as we were being reprimanded for not being more careful, the guys remained silent. I finally spoke up when I realized no one else would. I informed the executive director that I did not give her or anyone permission to deduct money from my check. If money were deducted, I would consider it theft and contact the corporate office and an employment lawyer. I proceeded to pull out the signed receipt book showing that money did not come up missing on my shift, but not without me taking extra measures.

As a result of speaking up, I was pulled into a meeting with the executive director and an associate director later that afternoon. They tried to guilt me into allowing them to take money from my check by questioning my loyalty to the team. I stressed that I went above and beyond to do what the organization failed to do, despite their awareness of this issue for months and their inaction to prevent it. I requested reimbursement for the safe I purchased and proposed that they keep the money in the nurse's office, where there is a secure safe with limited access and a camera. They, unfortunately, still pulled money from the other leaders' checks except mine. They reimbursed me for the safe I purchased, which was placed in the leaders' office. Additionally, they developed a new process and agreed to move the money to the nurse's station.

My relationship with the other leaders was affected, but not to the point where we weren't professional with one another. I was honest with them. I shared that I felt they should have spoken up for themselves. I shared my unwillingness to be a voice for someone who wouldn't use theirs when they were senior to me. While we continued to work well together, it was clear I would not be an unquestioningly accepting member of the group. The leader, whom we all suspected was stealing, was fired shortly after. I believe it was because he was caught (on camera) on the premises after hours multiple times.

At the time of this incident, I wasn't thinking about being an ethical leader or leading with integrity. I just knew wrong was wrong, and I wouldn't accept it silently. I did not consider the risks I exposed myself to. Realistically, I could have been fired for insubordination and experienced severe backlash from my peers because I didn't go along with the group's status quo - being excluded from paying the total cost of the stolen money. This was the first time in my career I had to stand up for myself and stay true to my inherent values. I believe this incident laid the foundation for me to continue to speak up for myself. I acknowledged the fear I felt as I confronted the leader during my shift, but I was determined not to show it because I knew I was right.

In conversations with two of my colleagues, I asked why they didn't speak up. One said it wasn't worth the risk of getting on the wrong side of the executive director and rocking the boat as he had a family to feed. He respected my decision, though. My other colleague didn't care. He had another job and a business, and this was a means to make extra money. He wouldn't have even noticed the amount they were taking after taxes. He said I should not have said anything and quit working so hard to improve things because the organization didn't care about me. I didn't realize it , but he had set clear boundaries for this position, and his core values differed significantly from mine. This showed me that there are many reasons why a person may not speak up. We all have different ethical compasses that we choose to adhere to.

※ ※ ※

VI.

Organizational culture is an organization's collective shared values, beliefs, attitudes, and behaviors. The significance of culture within an organization should never be underestimated, especially when you're attempting to solution complex business problems, because culture guides the interactions and drives decisions of its employees at all levels. How do business problems become complex? Do they start as large complex problems? No. They are typically a minor simple problem or a collection of interdependent, smaller, simple issues that are either not taken seriously or ignored and allowed to fester until they become a challenge to solution.

In the context of organizational culture, understanding the *why* behind how simple problem(s) remain un-solutioned will provide you with insight into how an organization approaches solutioning problems. Logically, an organization will have persistent issues with complex business problems if there is a failure to understand the importance of solutioning simple problems before they morph into complex problems. Recall that an organization's culture drives decisions and guides employee interactions at all levels. If there is a gap, you will need to understand it and how to resolve it as quickly as possible.

CASE STUDY 4

The Impact of Silos on Organizational Culture

I worked at a drug treatment facility in the sales and marketing department. After a few months, I noticed that I never saw anyone working together, including the therapist. You are probably wondering why this is a problem for me. In all honesty, I am not a particularly social person and I prefer to have my lunch alone. Still, I understood back then the importance of therapists collaborating and learning different skills from each other to become better at their jobs. My hope was the more they engaged, the more they could share therapeutic best practices and be more successful in treating their clients. The higher the success rate, the more likely businesses would make referrals to the organization, and I could use this information for marketing and increasing sales.

Although this seems like a complex problem, I initially viewed this as a simple problem. The general culture for an outpatient therapist was to work in silos and focus on their treatment plans. The behaviors of employees confirmed this because people rarely spoke to or engaged with each other. We would pass each other in the hall and seldom say hello. My solution was twofold. I created a shared Excel spreadsheet and pre-populated it with some challenges a therapist told me they were experiencing. I shared the link with all outpatient therapists and asked them if they could review it and offer insight. I also created a list of all the therapists and made it a point to be in the office during lunchtime and invite two therapists who had things in common to eat with me. Within three months, the sub-culture within the outpatient group had changed significantly. Within a year, the treatment success rate began to increase slightly. I was not aware at the time my efforts to solution a simple problem were, in fact, me addressing a symptom of a larger complex problem. I subsequently learned through other departments that major clients blocked the organization from referrals because of their poor reputation and low success rate. Shockingly, the problem was not just for outpatient services, but all programs and services offered by the organization. We had a major problem on our hands, but we were able to begin the process of turning things around at the time of my exit. For example, some of the most profitable referring organizations had re-opened their referral list.

Imagine if this were allowed to fester. The organization's success rate and client services would likely not have improved. The therapists would possibly not have begun engaging with each other. The organization eventually would have gone out of business due to the lack of referrals. Because of the siloed nature of the organization's culture, leaders across departments were unaware that this was a collective problem.

Have you ever worked, or are you currently working, in an organization with this cultural dynamic? Imagine if leadership could not solve, let alone identify, multiple interrelated simple problems. How would they solve a complex one, especially if it has morphed from a series of simple problems, such as in Case Study 4?

Rather than being strictly black and white, healthy, or toxic, an organization's culture exists on the spectrum. As a leader, you hold the key to deciding the health of your organization's culture. You serve as the cornerstone with the power to mold the very essence of your organization's cultural fabric. This responsibility is paramount, and it's crucial that, as a leader, you remain mindful of the profound impact culture can have on determining your success.

Complex business problem solutioning begins with consistently understanding and knowing your organization's culture. This is no small feat. I have noticed when discussing organizational culture; the perception is that it is linear. Discussions are centered around the general culture when speaking with leaders and a sub-culture when speaking with employees.

An organization's culture falls within two categories: the general culture - also referred to as the collective culture - and various sub-cultures within the general culture. I am choosing to refrain from referring to the general culture as a collective culture because collective implies a 100% symbiotic relationship when this is not the case within the organizational culture. It is essential to understand the difference between the two categories; you must respect and be aware of the value and influence each will have on your ability to lead cross-functional teams to solution complex business problems.

Can you think of a complex business problem that only affects one department? In my experience, complex business problems tend to affect the overall general culture and, as a result, may negatively impact some sub-cultures within the general culture. Some sub-cultures are not affected by the complex problem's existence. In some cases, some sub-cultures can benefit from the symptoms of a complex business problem. The challenge you will face as a leader is to influence these departments to make changes when the changes do not benefit them directly. In fact, at times, the changes may be an inconvenience to them.

Think of an organization's general culture as the architecture and design of an entire office building. It's the blueprint that shapes the overall look, feel, and functionality of the space, from the layout of the floors to the color scheme and decor. Just as the architecture sets the tone for the entire building, the general culture is the organization's public face. It shapes external perceptions among customers, stakeholders, and the broader public. The external image reflects the organization's identity and influences how it's perceived by those who interact with it, including customers, investors, and the community at large.

Now, envision the sub-cultures within the organization as different departments or divisions within that office building. Each department has its own distinct office layout, workspace setup, and team dynamics tailored to suit its specific needs and functions. Similarly, sub-cultures emerge within these departments, representing unique variations of the general culture influenced by factors such as team dynamics, leadership styles, and shared experiences. These sub-cultures add depth to the overall cultural landscape of the organization, much like how different departments contribute to the functionality and vitality of an office building.

The key here is to understand that while the general culture of an organization can be healthy, there can be toxic sub-cultures within the general culture and vice versa. As a leader, it is imperative that you not only embody TAAP™ as you are shaping the general culture of your organization, but also build relationships with leaders within the various sub-cultures to shape and influence those cultures as well. The stronger the relationships you have with the leaders and employees within each sub-culture, the more success you will have when solutioning complex business problems.

I am not suggesting that you need to know every single sub-culture within your organization; this will depend on the size of your organization and your role as a leader. You should assess which departments you impact, which impact you, and those with input and outputs to your department. This assessment will allow you to focus your efforts where they are most needed while facilitating collaboration and alignment across the organization. By starting with a foundational understanding, you can strategically navigate the complexities of your organization's culture. Through communication and collaboration, you can drive change and potentially solution simple problems before they morph into complex ones.

CASE STUDY 5

Unveiling the layers of corporate culture

An e-commerce giant, Amazon, is a household name and has become synonymous with convenience, innovation, and efficiency. Founder Jeff Bezos built the organization on the premise of an unwavering commitment to customer satisfaction to the point of obsession and high standards. With this focus, Amazon has maintained a reputation for exceeding customer expectations and delivering exceptional experiences. The organization accomplished this through a culture that is relentlessly customer-centric and data-driven.

Amazon's relentless pursuit of efficiency led to industry innovations such as Prime delivery and cashier-less stores, reshaping the retail landscape. Overall, Amazon increased the global accessibility and convenience of nearly all products in every industry.

From 1994 until mid-2010, Amazon maintained its public perception of its general culture until rumblings began to emerge that the organization's ability to maintain this relentless drive for innovation and customer obsession came at the expense of its employees' well-being. Reports of long working hours, intense productivity demands, inadequate breaks, and workplace safety concerns began to emerge. The media started to question what the human costs of Amazon's success were.

In August 2015, the New York Times published an article titled "Inside Amazon: Wrestling Big Ideas in a Bruising Workplace." This article peeled back the veil of Amazon's general culture rooted in excellence, efficiency, and innovation. It highlighted the impact of the general culture on the various departments within the organization. It also sheds light on the intense, demanding work environment within Amazon, showcasing high-pressure performance expectations and a culture of competition. It raised concerns about the impact of Amazon's work practices on employee well-being and sparked a widespread debate about the organization's general culture.

Interestingly, the article also inadvertently depicted the dangers of a company being too customer-centric! It highlighted the difference between the various sub-cultures and how they each aligned with the general culture. For example, it was found that teams working in corporate departments such as Amazon Web Services (AWS) or Alexa sub-cultures were more aligned with the organization's general culture than others. Their sub-culture, which was more creative and less laborious, was rooted in innovation and customer obsession. This drove these teams to push the boundaries of what's possible. Ironically, departments focusing on logistics, fulfillment, and more physically demanding labor faced intense pressure to meet targets. These departments also had a culture of high stress and burnout.

Each sub-culture had its priorities of delivery, which sometimes conflicted with the organization's general culture and resulted in internal conflicts. For example, although all departments worked towards meeting the needs of the same customer, some may have prioritized short-term results to address immediate needs, while others focused on long-term sustainability and innovation. This disparity caused inter-departmental conflicts.

In any organization, leadership's responsibility extends beyond overseeing day-to-day operations; it involves upholding the ethical standards and values that define the organization. As leaders, it's crucial to speak up when we see the drive to meet the organization's core values veer into the unethical treatment of employees in pursuit of its vision. Without careful monitoring and adjustments, these values risk being compromised and undermining the very foundation of the organization.

Amazon leaders must guarantee that the organization's core values of customer obsession, innovation, and high standards are upheld across all departments and teams to ensure the company can meet customer expectations, maintain its reputation, and achieve a profitable bottom line. It's also imperative they respect and value the subcultures within the organization because they have emerged to meet the demands of the general culture. Leaders must strike a delicate balance, addressing the diverse needs and priorities of different teams while maintaining alignment with the overarching goals of Amazon. Neglecting to address issues such as worker welfare or ethical concerns within specific sub-cultures has tarnished Amazon's reputation and undermined the organization's long-term success. Therefore, ethical leadership and a commitment to fostering a positive and inclusive general culture are paramount for Amazon's continued growth and impact in the global marketplace.

From 2010 to the present day, Amazon has grappled with a plethora of lawsuits from current and former employees citing grievances such as unsafe working conditions, inadequate breaks, discrimination, and unpaid wages. One notable incident occurred in 2018 when the Occupational Safety and Health Administration (OSHA) imposed fines totaling $28,000 against Amazon for alleged safety violations at a fulfillment center in New Jersey. This followed an incident where an employee sustained a finger injury while operating a conveyor belt. Among the cited violations were failures to provide adequate protections for employees working near conveyor belts and a lack of procedures to prevent machinery from starting up unexpectedly during maintenance. Despite contesting the fines and maintaining its innocence, Amazon's handling of such cases underscores ongoing concerns about workplace safety in its fulfillment centers and the regulatory scrutiny it faces.

Leadership within Amazon, like any sizable organization, is not a solitary endeavor. Drawing from the analogy of the office building with its various departments, each segment of Amazon's operations is overseen by at least one leader tasked with its management and direction.

Reflecting on Case Study 5, it's essential to consider the added layer of complexity that arises when leaders must collaborate and engage with one another. How can leaders effectively collaborate if the organization has internal competition? The challenges met by Amazon's leadership may reflect those you are currently navigating or will experience as a leader. The imperative lies in proactively strategizing your approach to solution complex business problems and swiftly confront any potential or clear unethical behavior.

As companies like Amazon navigate the intricacies of their cultural landscape, they must reconcile their core values with the relentless pursuit of innovation, to prioritize employee well-being and ethical integrity. This entails leaders adopting a holistic approach and shifting their mindset to integrate ethical considerations into their decision-making processes. They must foster a culture of open communication where employees feel empowered to raise concerns. Additionally, leaders should demonstrate their commitment to creating a positive and inclusive workplace culture by leading by example, all while simultaneously meeting their customers' needs. Continuous evaluation and improvement are also essential, ensuring that policies and practices align with core values and evolve to meet the changing needs of employees.

If Amazon prioritized its employees' evolving needs, it would foster a positive workplace culture while remaining true to its core value of a customer-centric approach. Afterall, satisfied and engaged employees are better equipped to deliver exceptional experiences to customers. Ultimately, it's through your actions and decisions as a leader that you shape the culture of your organization and leave a lasting impact on those you lead.

⚙ ⚙ ⚙

VII.

When an organization's core values diverge from its general culture, it can lead to significant challenges. At the general level, where the misalignment is more pervasive, it can indicate fundamental issues. It may manifest as confusion around priorities, decision-making paralysis, lack of purpose, or clarity of organizational goals. This misalignment becomes even more grave when sub-cultures exhibit behavioral inconsistencies, disengagement, communication breakdowns, resistance to change, high turnover rates, inequality, and customer dissatisfaction. These signals undermine employee morale, trust, and organizational effectiveness, potentially resulting in decreased productivity, increased turnover, and a damaged reputation. Addressing such issues requires a

53

comprehensive evaluation of the organization's core values and culture, followed by concerted efforts from leadership to bridge the gap, redefine core values, foster inclusivity, and promote alignment throughout the organization.

As a leader and business owner, I have come to realize the profound impact that core values have had on my personal growth and professional development. I came to this realization while working at an organization where the senior leadership's decisions did not align with the organization's general culture and many of its subcultures. For example, one of the core values was excellence. Yet, I never heard any leader, except for one, utter this word or exhibit behavior to indicate they were striving to achieve excellence. Leadership focused on survival to maintain its lead in the market as more agile competitors entered the industry with innovative products. They did this through speed without planning, metrics without validation, and solutions without industry-recognized methodologies.

Shockingly, this was the first time I worked for an organization that did not have a structured process for initiating, executing, and closing projects. Competing sub-cultures would not align to create a single process, although they were all working to deliver the same product to market. Everyone accepted that most projects failed and that the financial tracking of these projects was always questionable. However, without valid methods, they had no idea of the overall impact on the organization. A common statement was, 'We are constantly trying to build the plane while it is already in flight,' but no leader offered a solution. Lower-level employees were split. Some were in survival mode and adjusted their behavior to their respective leadership groups' expectations and seemed to be rewarded for not rocking the boat. Others challenged what appeared to be a 'good is good enough' attitude and were eventually laid off or became tired and quit.

This was the first time I've ever witnessed a great resignation of this magnitude. I don't know the exact numbers, but at least one hundred employees left within a few months. So much so that one department was severely understaffed, putting the organization at risk. Several projects were either canceled or placed on hold. In one instance, a colleague was doing the work of three different roles. Have you ever experienced a great resignation? Have you ever been a part of a great resignation? The caliber of employees the organization lost is a blow from which I doubt it will ever fully recover from. It's not just a matter of the quality of those who departed but also a reflection on who remained and why.

Whether it is the organization's core values or our own, they serve as a moral compass to empower us to remain true to ourselves. That said, before I partner with a potential client, we discuss our core values. This helps to gauge if they're a good fit. If they are not, I will not accept them as a client because not only will I be compromising my work ethic, but I would also be doing a disservice to the client.

EXCELLENCE

PERSONAL GROWTH

ETHICAL INTEGRITY

MY

SELF ACCOUNTABILITY

CORE VALUES

CLEAR COMMUNICATION

EMPOWERMENT

COLLABORATION

SELF AWARENESS

My core values are self-accountability and ethical integrity, clear communication and collaboration, self-awareness and personal growth, and empowerment and excellence. These values permeate this book as they are who I am. I'm committed to upholding them, no matter the consequences. They serve as my guiding principles and influence my decisions and how I interact with others. For example, I will not work with clients unwilling to empower their employees. While some may find it unconventional, I firmly adhere to the principle. As my grandmother would say, "All money ain't good money." My services would conflict with the organization's culture and how they do business, given that my approach is Agile, and to implement Agile services, you need empowered employees.

By defining my core values, I have empowered myself to be the leader I would want to have. My core values serve as my personal roadmap, guiding me to become the transformational leader I aspire to be on my terms. They are tangible and embody my commitment to cultivating genuine relationships free from the constraints of micromanagement and fear.

Can you see the power in defining your core values? Even if you are not a leader in an organization, this absolutely applies to you. Regardless of your role as an entrepreneur, leader, or employee, defining your core values is essential in your journey to self-empowerment and embodying TAAP™. Core-value development is not limited to organizations and leaders alone; it is equally necessary for employees. As members of cross-functional teams, aligning core values fosters healthy relationships with both leaders and peers. An employee whose core values clash with the organization's core values may be change-averse and can hinder or delay efforts to solution complex business problems. That said, encourage employees to define their core values within a team. Cohesive teams, aligned with the core values of an organization, are positioned to solution complex business problems effectively.

I am often baffled when leaders ask, "How do we empower employees?" The solution is simple: get out of their way and provide the support and tools necessary for them to learn to empower themselves. I believe the same logic applies to leaders. Leaders should focus on developing the *what* and providing a vision while allowing employees to define the *how*. This autonomy requires sufficient resources and fosters creativity and collaboration across all levels of the organization, regardless of the role. I'm not suggesting that leaders shouldn't be involved in defining the *how*; instead, their role should shift to offering support, guidance, and resources versus giving instructions and assignments. Building a culture built on respect, trust, and self-empowerment on both ends is essential to achieving the desired outcomes when solutioning complex business problems.

I understand the struggle to remain committed and do the right thing, even under challenging circumstances. Whether it's the risk of losing your job, facing ostracism from peers, or knowing that the right thing may require extra effort. The decision weighs heavily. Regardless of your choice, as a leader, I implore you to hold yourself accountable. If you find yourself in a room full of peers and sense something is amiss, be bold and speak up. Don't succumb to peer pressure or politics. Instead, consider the holistic impact your decisions will have on the organization and employees who trust you. If you choose not to say anything, please hold yourself accountable when a problem rears its ugly head because of your and your peers' inaction.

It's your responsibility to empower yourself and become the leader you would want to have and the leader your employees strive to be. Remember, this is a personal journey. Don't judge yourself. Be transparent and honest. It's about the journey, not the destination or roadblocks. Keep striving for growth and authenticity. Reflect on the significance of your core values; write them down! They serve as an integral compass, providing you with a roadmap to align with your organizational values and guide your decisions as an ethical leader.

VIII.

Understanding an organization's business practices offers valuable insight into its culture, operations, core values, and priorities. As we have established, general culture plays a pivotal role in an organization's success and longevity, and core values are the bedrock of the organization's culture. However, unthinkingly following core values can lead to ethical dilemmas. If it appears that in the pursuit of achieving an organization's core value, you will cross the line of ethics, be the empowered leader who raises a red flag to ensure sufficient time to correct the course. Ethical leadership entails taking accountability for creating a work environment where employees are physically and psychologically safe.

Core values can serve as a powerful tool to enhance transparency and visibility within your organization. There are three types of core values that can be used to facilitate cultural alignment across the primary levels in your organization. The three types are enterprise, management, and employee. You are uniquely positioned to establish this visibility as a leader, offering three distinct advantages. Firstly, core values promote alignment by unifying individuals and teams with the organization's overarching mission. Secondly, core values offer clarity by defining expected actions and promoting consistency in decision-making and behavior across the organization. Finally, core values enhance accountability and performance as employees hold themselves and others accountable for upholding these values in their daily work, driving improved performance and organizational success.

ENTERPRISE

EMPLOYEE

MANAGMENT

CORE VALUES

Enterprise Core Values (Level One): Foundational beliefs and principles set up by senior leadership that define the organization's identity and guide decision-making at all levels. They serve as the bedrock of the company and are deeply ingrained in the general culture. They shape every aspect of operations, fostering a sense of purpose and direction.

Management Core Values (Level Two): Individual beliefs within each department influence how managers lead and align the overarching enterprise values with their personal core values. These values reflect the subculture in each department and manifest in their unique leadership styles by providing guidance, clarity, and accountability. This alignment ensures consistency and effectiveness in leadership practices to fulfill departmental goals and drive enterprise-level strategic objectives while also serving as a guiding compass for employees.

Employee Core Values (Level Three): Personal beliefs and core values that guide employees' actions and attitudes. Alignment of these personal core values with Level One and Level Two core values is essential to ensure a harmonious work environment. They ensure the sub-culture is designed to drive both departmental goals in Level Two and the strategic objectives in Level One,.

While some may perceive this approach as too demanding or impractical, the return on investment outweighs the time and resource efforts invested. You are creating a process that paves the way for cross-functional support and collaboration. I encourage you to work with your teams to not only define your core values but write them out, collaborate with other departments to assess them for multi-departmental alignment, and establish a regular review process to ensure alignment is maintained.

Let's take a moment to reflect on the layers of complexity associated with defining your core values at all organizational levels, how these core values shape organizational culture, and the level of ethics leaders are expected to uphold. The journey to becoming an ethical leader is undeniably challenging. It is not simply about what is right or wrong. It requires you to TAAP™ into your personal and organizational core values while also being adaptable, empathetic, and understanding of employees' core values. This involves navigating environments where personal values may not always align with colleagues, subordinates,' or an organization's core values. This delicate balance cannot be taught in a class; it is learned through self-awareness and experience. Making a personal commitment to defining what ethical leadership means to you and establishing clear boundaries based on your definition of ethical and unethical is essential on this journey. It is profoundly personal and integral to your self-development as a leader capable of purposefully disrupting the status quo and effectively solutioning complex business problems.

VIIII.

To unethical leaders, I urge you to consider the long-term repercussions of your actions. While choosing to go against company values may offer short-term gains, it inevitably leads to an erosion of trust, a damaged reputation, and potential legal consequences. By embracing ethical leadership, you not only pave the way for personal success but also safeguard your organization's integrity and the stability of its employees. This commitment fosters a sustainable culture, which is essential for long-term prosperity. Moreover, it strategically positions your organization to navigate challenges effectively, creating an environment where complex business problems can be solutioned.

True leadership isn't just about making ethical choices; it's about illuminating the path with integrity and guiding others towards the beacon of what's right. Leading with integrity requires dedication and a deliberate commitment to uphold your personal and organizational core values. It involves continuous self-reflection and growth. Additionally, understanding your leadership style is essential, as it provides insight into your strengths, weaknesses, and areas for improvement. By understanding who you are as a leader and the style you naturally lean towards, you can use this information as a baseline to develop strategies and set goals to enhance your integrity and effectiveness.

Enhancing your integrity involves defining your core values and consistently checking and adjusting them as you mature as a leader. You should also commit to developing a continuous learning routine of consistent self-reflection and awareness. You will achieve a greater sense of authenticity in your leadership style while striving to be an effective and adaptable leader capable of transforming, aligning, adapting, and pivoting (TAAPing) through organizational and market changes.

COMPLEXITIES OF LEADERSHIP

I.

Contrary to popular belief, not everyone can be an effective leader, let alone an exceptional one. Leadership isn't a one-size-fits-all skill; it comes more naturally to some while requiring diligent effort from others. Take a moment to consider the different types of leaders:

- Isabella, a natural-born leader, has charisma and confidence that effortlessly commands her team's attention. She falls into the first category of individuals with leadership potential—those whose personality types naturally embody the skills essential for effective leadership.

- Benjamin possesses some necessary leadership personality traits but hasn't fully realized his leadership potential yet. With dedication and cultivation, he can become an effective leader.

- Gracelynn, an introvert with a reserved personality, may not naturally align with traditional leadership traits. However, with considerable effort and self-awareness, she, too, can develop the skills needed to lead effectively.

Greatness isn't just about the talents you're born with; it's about using those talents to reach new heights of excellence. Whether you're naturally inclined to lead or not, what truly matters is the effort you invest in becoming the leader you aspire to be. Acknowledging self-leadership development as a lifelong journey is vital. It is a commitment to mastering the intricacies of leadership and adopting a growth mindset. By embracing this discipline, we can all work towards becoming more impactful leaders in our respective industries.

Just a quick note before we proceed, within the *Escaping the Hamster Wheel* companion workbook, you'll uncover a wealth of resources meticulously crafted to enrich your leadership journey. As you continue your journey through the pages of this book, I encourage you to work with the companion workbook simultaneously. You'll engage in a series of assessments designed with your growth in mind. These assessments converge to form what I've dubbed the VIGLS leadership assessment—a beacon guiding you toward a deeper understanding of your 'self' and your unique leadership qualities. Through this process, you'll remain vigilant cultivating the tools and resources needed to enhance your leadership potential!

Consider the type of leader you identify with from the examples above and your plans to develop your leadership skills further. Remember, we all start somewhere. This is not a competition. We often view our leadership style as fixed, but it's more accurately considered inherently fluid. There isn't a single assessment that can definitively pinpoint your leadership style. Instead, leadership style assessments offer insights based on self-perception and external perceptions. These assessments may be skewed due to various factors. Research indicates that situational demands, follower characteristics, and personal growth all contribute to shaping your leadership style. It all comes down to personality. While recognizing that your inherent leadership style is valuable, treating leadership styles as a discipline to master is equally beneficial. After all, adjusting one's personality can be a significant challenge.

Effective leaders can remarkably adapt their style to meet the unique demands of changing environments. Like chameleons who adjust their color to blend in, adaptive leaders modify their approach while maintaining their core principles and values. This flexibility empowers them to navigate challenges, inspire their teams, and drive success without compromising integrity. Effective leaders excel at flexibly adjusting their style while remaining grounded.

II.

Leadership styles are not prescriptive. They do not dictate rigid behaviors that you must follow to execute. They are frameworks that guide how to approach and interact with your team. While each style may have its recommended practices, all are flexible in their application. Meaning, although you can master learning what style may work best in a specific environment or scenario, the success in its delivery boils down to your level of empathy, communication skills, and, most importantly, your personality.

The more skills you acquire, the more effective as a leader you'll be. Sounds easy, right? Well, not so much. Mastering leadership styles can be likened to advancing through the different levels of martial arts, requiring dedication and continuous effort. In martial arts, beginners start with a white belt, symbolizing a blank canvas or a foundation upon which to build their skills. Similarly, novice leaders may begin with a basic understanding of leadership styles, perhaps favoring one or two styles that align with their natural tendencies or initial training. As martial artists progress, they earn colored belts that represent a deeper level of knowledge, proficiency, and mastery. Likewise, as leaders develop their skills, they expand their repertoire of leadership styles, becoming proficient in adapting their approach to different situations and team dynamics. Just as martial artists must practice and refine their techniques to advance to higher belt levels, leaders must continuously hone their leadership skills. They must learn to leverage different leadership styles strategically.

Ultimately, achieving the coveted black belt in martial arts is like mastering leadership styles, which signifies an advanced level of proficiency and versatility. Leaders who attain this level possess a deep understanding of themselves, their team members, and the nuances of leadership. This mastery enables them to navigate complex business problems with skill, grace, and effectiveness. But it does not stop there! Leadership development is an ongoing journey that spans a lifetime. Mastering various leadership styles is merely a stepping stone in this journey. That said, remain open to continuous exploration. Seek new techniques, styles, and philosophies to refine your leadership skills. This may involve learning different disciplines, asking advice from mentors, and/or participating in training and workshops.

III.

Eight widely recognized leadership styles have undergone extensive examination and analysis in various sectors, academic fields, and corporate environments. These styles have been subject to thorough research, demonstrating their significant impact on a leader's overall efficacy. Many leadership theories and frameworks are constructed around these foundational styles. They encompass a range of approaches that leaders can utilize to inspire their teams. Evolving, they have been influenced by different theories, philosophies, and organizational needs.

As a leader, I advocate for mastering each leadership style as it enhances one's versatility. Not all styles are equally suited for every situation. Each style has its purpose, and its efficacy can vary depending on the context and audience. With that in mind, let's examine which leadership style is most effective for solutioning complex business problems.

Autocratic leadership is characterized by centralized decision-making with minimal input from team members, making it practical for quick decision-making scenarios. Nevertheless, it often leaves team members feeling disempowered with limited opportunities for creativity, autonomy, and personal growth. When solutioning complex business problems, there are times when centralized decision-making from a leader is required. Still, it should be kept to a minimum and only used when something may be a distraction if brought to the team.

Democratic leadership fosters collaboration and participation among team members in decision-making, promoting engagement and commitment. However, if not executed effectively, it can result in disagreements due to diverse perspectives. Without a middle ground, there is a risk of mediocrity due to compromising on solutions. When tackling complex business problems, a diverse, self-empowered team with multidisciplinary skills is essential. The extent of team empowerment is contingent on various factors, including inclusivity and openness in decision-making.

This process often favors assertive or influential individuals on the team, leading to unequal participation and selective empowerment of members. While members may be empowered on the surface, their effectiveness in solutioning complex business problems depends on the leader's ability to manage diverse perspectives and ensure that all voices are heard and valued.

Laissez-faire leadership, which translates to "let do" or "let go," grants significant autonomy to team members, empowering them to make decisions independently. This approach relies heavily on trusting team members to fulfill their assigned tasks autonomously. However, when it comes to solutioning complex business problems, a collaborative effort between the leader and the team is essential. In such scenarios, the leader must actively provide support and guidance while removing any impediments that could distract the team from the complex problem solutioning process. While a hands-off approach can empower self-motivated team members to thrive, it also carries inherent risks. Without clear accountability and guidance, there is a potential for inaction and lack of progress.

Transactional leadership emphasizes exchanges between leaders and followers with clear expectations, rewards for meeting goals, and consequences for failure to ensure goal attainment. Transactional leaders tend to lean towards micromanaging to account for rewards and punishments. This style is unsuitable for complex business problem solutioning because it does not allow for the self-empowerment of a team, and it often prioritizes short-term goals over long-term strategic thinking. This risk-adverse approach disempowers the team from taking calculated risks and exploring unconventional and innovative solutions, which are crucial elements when solutioning complex business problems.

Situational leadership underscores the importance of adjusting leadership approaches to fit the specific circumstances and team members' readiness. This adaptive leadership style requires flexibility, agility, and the ability to effectively navigate various challenges and uncertainties. Situational leaders carefully assess the context and consider factors such as the complexity of the problem, the skills of team members, and the dynamics of the situation. They adapt their leadership style to match the demands of the situation and the developmental level of their team members. However, situational leaders may face challenges in accurately assessing their existing team's skill level.

Misjudging the readiness level or applying the wrong leadership style can lead to ineffective communication, goal misalignment, and reduced team participation. Therefore, situational leaders must continuously monitor their approach based on real-time feedback to ensure that the team is adequately equipped to solution complex business problems.

Servant leadership calls for leaders who place a strong emphasis on creating an environment in which team members are supported, valued, and encouraged to contribute their ideas and perspectives. Servant leaders prioritize the growth and development of team members and foster a sense of community and collaboration. While this approach is known for promoting empowerment and shared decision-making, it can pose challenges when it comes to solutioning complex business problems.

The emphasis on inclusivity and collaboration can lead to challenges in balancing the needs of multiple stakeholders, especially when conflicts arise regarding the team's approach or accountability. In addition, adopting a servant leadership approach may sometimes create a perception of lower authority, making it difficult to assert boundaries or address behaviors that require firm action. Servant leaders need to find a balance between meeting the needs of their team members while maintaining their authority.

Charismatic leadership involves leaders with compelling personalities that inspire loyalty and devotion. Charismatic leaders often rally others around their vision. They excel at building trust, fostering open communication, and creating a supportive team environment where diverse perspectives are valued and encouraged. Their infectious energy and charisma can motivate team members to think outside the box, take risks, and push the boundaries of conventional thinking in search of innovative solutions. By leveraging their influence, they can bridge divides and break down barriers among cross-functional team members with different backgrounds, expertise, and viewpoints.

Although charismatic leadership can play a significant role in complex business problem solutioning, being charismatic is not enough. Often, this style is leveraged with another style, such as servant leadership or transformational leadership. Charismatic leaders must have a balance between inspiring a team and providing the necessary guidance and resources to translate their vision into actionable strategies.

IV.

As you can see, within the realms of leadership, there are a variety of leadership styles available to ensure success. Each has its own unique approach, application, and benefits. However, when it comes to solutioning complex business problems, one style stands out above the rest, and it is transformational leadership.

Transformational leadership, one of the most common leadership styles spoken about today, was initially developed by James MacGregor Burns in his book *Leadership*. Unlike the other styles that focus on maintaining stability or achieving specific goals, transformational leadership is characterized by its ability to inspire and motivate team members to reach extraordinary heights. This style prioritizes vision, inspiration, empowerment, and emotional intelligence. Transformational leaders are uniquely positioned to drive organizational change and solution complex business problems.

The transformative leadership style exhibits a remarkable synergy with Agile methodologies. Both transformational leaders and Agile leaders share characteristics that effectively align the leader's role with the team's functions. While the concept of an Agile team or leader didn't emerge until the early 2000s, the agile nature of transformational leadership was evident long before, demonstrating foresight on the part of pioneers like Mr. MacGregor in 1978.

The primary distinction between a transformational leader and an Agile leader lies in the approach versus mindset. An Agile leader doesn't merely adopt a particular approach but embraces a mindset rooted in agility, flexibility, and adaptability to change. They prioritize collaboration, iteration, and continuous improvement. They aim to deliver value swiftly and iteratively. They empower teams to self-organize and make autonomous decisions. Agile leadership is more than a style— it becomes the very essence of leadership for an Agile leader; it is who they are.

Conversely, transformational leaders inspire through vision and purpose, fostering individual growth, innovation, and a culture of trust. While they may adapt their style to various situations, their focus remains on driving organizational change and surpassing expectations. Despite their differences, Agile and Transformational leadership can coexist synergistically. An Agile leader can embody transformative qualities by motivating their team to embrace Agile principles, work towards common goals, and drive organizational change by solutioning complex business problems. Combining the agility of Agile leadership with the transformative nature of transformational leadership yields a new potent leadership approach: a **Transformative Agile**™ **Leadership Style**.

Agile leaders who embrace the Transformative Agile™ Leadership Style can nurture high-performing teams and ensure that their teams are continually evolving through individual growth and development initiatives. By nurturing each team member's personal and professional development— which is not currently a focus of Agile leadership—Agile leaders embrace an elevated culture of continuous improvement, sustainability, and innovation within the team.

The dual emphasis on team collaborative performance and individual growth empowers Agile leaders to cultivate teams that thrive in adaptability, responsiveness, and a dedication to excellence. Ultimately, this approach creates self-evolving teams equipped to solution complex business problems. When discussing a high-performing team, I'm referring to a collective group empowered by Agile leadership, principles, and a commitment to individual growth—an idea pioneered by Patrick Lencioni in 2002, now a benchmark for team excellence. Leaders who adopt the Transformative Agile™ leadership style should aim to continuously TAAP™ into the team's collective advancement and individual members' development. This involves foreseeing the need to pivot in the future and ensuring someone on the team is actively developing those skills.

For many, forming a high-performing team begins with setting clear expectations. However, it might come as a surprise to learn that while building self-evolving teams uniquely adept at solutioning complex business problems, these initial actions serve as a fraction of the foundation required. Additional steps are necessary to ensure sustained success.

V.

Often hailed as the father of modern management, Peter Drucker challenged common stereotypes associated with leadership. While charisma and influence are often emphasized, Drucker highlighted deeper qualities that define effective leadership. For instance, while leaders may have these characteristics, they are not the sole determinants of effectiveness. Authentic leadership, according to Drucker, transcends individual traits. It involves inspiring team members beyond current capabilities to strive for higher goals. Leadership can sometimes be misinterpreted as manipulative or self-serving, aimed at garnering personal favor. However, genuine leadership is not about personal qualities but rather about a leader's impact on others.

While I wholeheartedly agree with Drucker's perspective, I also believe that effective leadership requires a deep understanding of oneself. It is crucial to recognize one's personality traits and how they can either propel or hinder one's impact on others. It's not about being liked; it's about having the self-awareness and confidence to persevere through challenges and lead with conviction.

Candace Owens, a prominent Black conservative commentator and activist, has a dynamic personality and the ability to influence others through her assertive communication style. Whether loved or hated her effectiveness as a leader goes beyond these traits. Owens demonstrates authentic leadership by challenging conventional narratives, inspiring others to think critically, and advocating for the causes she believes in. Despite facing backlash and criticism, not only from liberal commentators and organizations but from most of the Black community who disagree with her views and feel she does not adequately represent their interests or experiences, the opposition underscores her conviction in her beliefs. She is so confident that she often engages in discussions with those who oppose her views. Imagine being so confident in what you believe that you are willing to have an open, productive, and respectful conversation with those who oppose you.

As you continue this journey toward shifting your mindset, the Enneagram Assessment is a tool that can provide a transformative experience and offer profound insights into your personality, motivations, and behaviors. Rooted in ancient wisdom yet profoundly relevant today, the Enneagram is a powerful tool used to understand yourself and others. Unlike traditional personality tests, the Enneagram delves into nine distinct personality types, focusing on underlying motivations rather than surface traits. This assessment enables you to gain clarity on your strengths, weaknesses, and areas for growth as a leader. This is a valuable tool for personal and team development.

Using Candace Owens as an example, her unwavering confidence and tendency to challenge the status quo suggest traits resonating with Type 8: The Challenger, known for assertiveness and a desire for control; Type 3: The Achiever, characterized by ambition and a focus on success, and Type 7: The Enthusiast, marked by optimism and a thirst for new experiences While these are speculative based on her public persona, they underscore the professional benefits of having assertiveness, ambition, and optimism. These traits enrich professional success by having the ability to foster effective communication, drive goal achievement, and cultivate resilience in demanding circumstances.

This assessment isn't meant to confine you within a rigid framework but rather offer insight into your leadership style and provide you with a baseline. Recognizing strengths and weaknesses is essential for growth, enabling you to address limitations effectively. Identifying your personality type is a crucial step in becoming a more effective leader. Comparing your traits against those of admired leaders can guide your path towards a desired leadership style. No one is perfect. Even the most adept leaders stumble—whether due to a mistake, error in judgment, or setback in their role. How they recover is key and is determined by how well their core values and personality align with their approach. Understanding the different leadership methodologies and striving to have the proper traits are crucial to becoming an effective leader capable of solutioning complex business problems.

VI.

Addressing conflict avoidance may not be a comfortable topic. However, it's essential to acknowledge its significance in your leadership journey. Conflict isn't about being aggressive; it's about addressing challenging issues and fostering open dialogue even when opinions differ. Again, Candace Owens actively engages in conflict as a catalyst for growth. While conflict may seem unsettling, it presents opportunities for progress.

Conflict-avoidant leaders may appear adept at mediating disputes on the surface, but they often prioritize superficial harmony over confronting the root cause of issues. Their focus on maintaining peace can lead to unresolved tensions that fester and escalate. This eventually damages morale, trust, and collaboration among team members. Depending on how they manage conflicts, these leaders may exhibit traits from various leadership styles, such as autocratic, laissez-faire, transactional, or even narcissistic. They will likely appear as Type 9: The Peacemaker on the Enneagram. They're characterized by a desire for inner peace, often avoiding conflict to maintain a sense of tranquility. They may struggle with assertiveness and confrontation, preferring to keep equilibrium within their environment. While they possess many positive qualities (e.g., empathy, diplomacy, etc.), their avoidance of conflict can hinder their ability to address critical issues directly. This stifles growth and innovation within the team.

Take a moment to reflect on your own experiences with conflict. Consider instances where you've refrained from raising significant concerns in meetings. When faced with discomfort, did you address the issue directly? Did you deflect? Or did you avoid it?

VII.

During my undergraduate years, I studied psychology and was introduced to the field of behavioral economics. I have always been curious about the psychology behind how and why people make their decisions and how external environmental pressures influence a person's decision-making. As I progressed in my career, I observed my leaders, made mental notes of their personalities, and tried to understand the reasons behind their decisions. Being curious, I would ask. It would either be received as me being insubordinate or as a potential leader with natural curiosity. My point is, I recognize that leaders are not always going to make unbiased, fair decisions that make sense.

Traditional economic theories before the 1970s were based on simplified models of human behavior. They assumed that individuals were rational beings who made decisions based on maximizing their utility or satisfaction, given their preferences for constraints. An excellent example of this theory is the Efficient Market Hypothesis (EMH), which states that rational leaders are logical. They weigh the pros and cons of every decision and act only after considering available information and evidence. They set aside personal needs, biases, and emotions in favor of objective assessment and critical thinking. Rational leaders prioritize data-driven decision-making and strive to make choices in the best interest of their organization, team, and stakeholders.

Rational leadership is about making tough decisions, driven by a commitment to doing what's right and guided by sound reasoning and information regardless of potential consequences. Rational leaders excel in solutioning complex business problems by adhering to industry best practices and guidelines. They embrace innovation and disruption. Found in fields like finance, engineering, science, law, business, and healthcare, rational leaders navigate complex challenges focusing on achieving optimal results.

Being a leader is not easy. As you progress in your career, you will face tough decisions, but it is essential to understand yourself and how you react to challenges. Let's look at this scenario of a leader faced with a complex business problem. Would you assume the approach of a rational leader, or would you focus on self-preservation?

SCENARIO 1

The CEO's Dilemma: Financial Survival vs. Well-Being

Imagine you're the CEO of a company facing a tough dilemma: your business is struggling financially, and you need to cut costs to stay afloat. You know that laying off employees is necessary to reduce expenses, but you also understand the human impact of these decisions. As a rational leader, you weigh the company's financial viability against the well-being of your employees.

Despite knowing that layoffs may lead to personal hardships for your team members, you recognize the need to make tough decisions for the organization's greater good. You carefully analyze data, consider alternative solutions, and consult with stakeholders to ensure your decision is grounded in logic and reason. However, as you announce the layoffs, you're met with resistance and backlash from employees who feel betrayed and undervalued. Despite your rational approach, emotions run high. Maintaining morale becomes a significant challenge. You grapple with feelings of guilt. You question whether there was a better way to manage the situation.

While rationality is a cornerstone of effective decision-making, you must recognize that authentic, genuine leadership involves navigating the complexities of human emotions and relationships. As a rational leader, you meticulously analyze data and consider alternatives, ultimately making tough decisions to ensure the company's survival. However, the human impact of these decisions cannot be overlooked.

Despite the rationality behind the layoffs (in the scenario), employees may feel undervalued and betrayed. This highlights the nuanced nature of leadership, where rationality must be balanced with empathy. Leaders must make data-driven decisions and understand and address the emotional implications for their team members. While rationality guides decision-making processes, effective leadership requires a holistic approach encompassing compassion and a deep understanding of human dynamics. By striking this balance, leaders can navigate challenges with integrity.

Reflecting on the scenario, while layoffs may seem like a rational cost-cutting measure, there could be alternative solutions within the organization. For instance, other departments may be actively hiring, presenting an opportunity to redeploy employees facing layoffs. As a rational leader, conducting a skill assessment of affected employees and matching their skills to open positions can be a proactive approach to mitigating the impact of layoffs. By offering employees the choice to transfer to other roles, leaders prove a commitment to both financial prudence and employee well-being. This underscores the significance of maintaining rationality in decision-making while also ensuring that the best interests of all stakeholders are considered.

❧ ❧ ❧

VIII.

It is far more challenging to be vulnerable with yourself than it is to be vulnerable with anyone else. Humans all wear a veil and keep a tiny part of us hidden from others, especially in professional settings. There is only one person on this earth from whom you cannot hide anything: yourself. The more authentic, honest, and committed you can be to yourself and your professional development, the more you will grow as a leader.

I recall the first time I went zip-lining—a thrilling yet nerve-wracking adventure that pushed me far beyond my comfort zone. As someone with an innate fear of heights, the idea of soaring through the air like a bird both excited and terrified me in equal measure. Little did I know the rollercoaster of emotions that awaited me.

As we climbed up the mountain, excitement tinged with trepidation coursed through my veins. As the ascent progressed, so did my mounting unease. The sheer height of the mountain seemed to grow with each step, and my confidence faltered. I had envisioned a leisurely ascent, but reality hit hard as the ground fell away beneath me. My attempt to maintain a facade of composure quickly unraveled. While the fearless children in our group effortlessly bounded up the mountain, I found myself lagging, clinging to a flimsy stick for support. My knees threatened to give way at any moment while hyperventilation set in, and panic tightened its grip.

Despite the urge to turn back, a stubborn determination rooted me in place. I couldn't bear the thought of admitting defeat, especially in front of my nieces, who watched my every move with amusement and concern. So, with shaky resolve, I soldiered on, fueled by embarrassment and unwavering determination. Finally, reaching the summit felt like a Herculean feat, but the actual test awaited - the descent. As my turn approached, a mix of emotions swirled within me: fear, excitement, and a tinge of reckless abandon. With a racing heart and trembling limbs, I took a leap of faith and hurtled into the abyss with a mix of terror and exhilaration.

The rush of wind against my face and adrenaline coursing through my veins was a sensation like no other! Each zip line on the descent down brought its own unique challenges, but with each plunge into the unknown, I felt a newfound sense of courage blossoming within me. As I landed safely at the bottom, my laughter mingled with relief as I realized I had conquered the mountain and my fears.

In the aftermath of the adventure, amidst the playful teasing of my nieces and the proud nods of the guides, I couldn't help but feel a sense of awe at what I had accomplished. Despite my lingering fear of heights, I refused to let it define me. I embraced the challenge head-on and emerged stronger and braver on the other side. The guides remarked, 'She is definitely the most afraid person to go up the mountain, but she was also the one that was the boldest once she jumped!'

The pressure to make pivotal decisions and deliver solutions can be overwhelming, especially when it involves solutioning complex business problems. A leader's ability to remain both rational and ethical is paramount. It is during this time that one should revisit their company's core values and decide which leadership style will work best to solution a complex business problem. Beyond contending with their own psychological biases, leaders must navigate a maze of variables and uncertainties inherent in the complex problem.

In addition, the pressure and sense of urgency to resolve the complex problem can reduce the likelihood of making an uninformed and, at times, disastrous decision. I have found it interesting that it is not always the senior leader who makes the most rational and informed decision; it is the leader with a wider breadth of tools who understands both the general and sub-cultures and has built genuine relationships across various levels of an organization.

I've witnessed the impact when a leader operates from a teacher-student dynamic driven by an unspoken fear of outcomes. These fears include the fear of reprimand, facing consequences for mistakes, becoming a scapegoat due to internal politics, or the failing to meet expectations regardless of the task's integrity. Additionally, leaders may fear their peers or subordinates will discover their limitations or outshine them. Such fears can undermine ethical leadership, as true integrity requires a foundation free from fear-based dynamics.

CASE STUDY 6

Navigating Uncharted Waters

New to my position as a leader in a technology organization, I oversaw project delivery and customer engagement. Soon after starting my position, I discovered a director — a long-standing employee and friend of the CEO had been engaging in unethical behavior. This director had added non-existent functionality to client contracts, accompanied by fabricated one-pagers explaining the features and associated costs. During an introductory meeting with a long-standing client, I noticed discrepancies in the functionality they claimed to have bought and had questions about a decision to move forward with the new enhanced feature at an added cost. Sensing something was amiss, I politely requested copies of the one-pagers for my records. I informed the client that I was unfamiliar with this functionality but would have a sales representative walk them through their options. I was new to the position and wasn't sure what to do without having built any relationships. I considered the potential consequences if I chose to ignore my suspicions. Also, I questioned myself. *If I choose to ignore these suspicions, what type of leader would this make me?*

Despite the potential discomfort and professional repercussions of confronting a senior colleague and friend of the CEO, I knew that silence was not an option. Armed with irrefutable evidence, I brought the issue to the attention of senior management who addressed the issue. I was even thanked for bringing it to their attention. I did not inquire further as to what the outcomes were regarding the accountability of senior-level staff, but within a day, an email went out informing all employees to quit using the one-pagers as new marketing materials would be provided within the week.

I knew, based on my core values and those of the company, that I made the right decision. My relationship with the senior-level leader was strained, but I worked hard to build strong relationships with other leaders and had no issues going forward. What was most valuable to me in this experience is that I had a few staff members privately thank me because they did not feel they had the authority to question their senior-level leader. An empowered team would have caught and addressed this unethical behavior before it ever reached a client, and no one would have felt pressured to take part in unethical activities.

Leading with integrity requires embracing your professional self-development as a life-long journey for which only you are accountable. It is about confronting uncomfortable truths while continuously advocating for what is right, even when it is easier to remain silent. It involves risks. It can be scary, but it builds credibility. Your commitment to leadership will only strengthen relationships and empower others to speak up immediately when they see a simple problem within the organization before it morphs into a complex problem.

THE ESSENCE OF LEADERSHIP

I.

Dr. W. Edwards Deming, the father of quality management systems, recognized fear-based leadership as having roots in the education system. According to Deming, there is a direct correlation between a boss-subordinate and a teacher-student relationship.

In a traditional teacher-student relationship, the teacher provides the vision and direction and has all the answers. The student follows the directions and does what the teacher tells them to do. But what happens when the student doesn't do what the teacher says or corrects the information the teacher has provided? Unless it is a forward-thinking teacher, the student risks getting in trouble. They could be singled out as being disruptive and given a consequence. They could be embarrassed if the teacher's response is defensive. They may not be rewarded for their insight and may be ostracized by their peers, even if their peers know the answer was correct as well. This teacher-student dynamic is built on the fear of getting in trouble and the strong desire to please the teacher at all costs. Interestingly, there are research articles providing support to students who find themselves in these types of situations and how to manage them.

How do you know when you've pleased the teacher? You may receive a high mark on your assignment, a good grade in your course, a certificate, verbal recognition, and maybe even praise in front of your parents. In the education system, there is blind trust in the teacher to know the correct answers, provide the best guidance, set the criteria for success, be fair, and recognize students who've met their criteria for success. There is also an awareness of negative consequences when expectations are unmet. Because teachers set the requirements, how can you challenge them when you know something is wrong? As a professional, does this sound familiar? The teacher is essentially performing the role of the boss!

I cringe when I hear someone refer to a leader as their boss. Firstly, they are ultimately saying, "Hi, this is Jim, who has complete control and authority over me." Secondly, given the history of enslavement, racism, and misogyny towards Black women in America and corporate environments, I refuse to identify myself as, or allow anyone to refer to me as, the boss.

II.

Historically, in business, I have found that leaders believe they should know the answers, and if they don't, they make it up. There is an assumption that leaders are like teachers, and their subordinates are there to carry out their vision and learn the answers along the way. In a teacher-student dynamic in business, the leader dictates how the vision is carried out, even if they have no experience in the subject matter. Experienced subordinates are subject matter experts selected based on their specific skill sets. However, they are often told what to do by a higher-ranking novice who has the power to make final decisions or by a former subject matter expert who has outdated experience in the field.

Like the teacher, the leader defines the criteria for success, and the subordinate performs tasks to meet the requirements. The subordinate must consistently report their progress to the leader, which can quickly morph into micromanagement. This results in the subject matter expert delivering to please the leader and not to create *value*. The subordinate essentially develops a tunnel-vision approach while completing the assigned tasks because, like the teacher, the leader is performing the role of a boss, and you don't question the boss. You complete assigned tasks.

What happens if you voice concerns or fail to deliver tasks by a set deadline? You may be ostracized by other teammates trying to gain the leader's favor or fit in with the group. You may receive a verbal or written reprimand. You may even experience the loss of a promotion or bonus, peer isolation, and so on. What do you do if you know the answer or approach the leader has provided is wrong? In my experience, the higher the rank of the leader, the more likely the employee will perform the task, knowing it is wrong. They will not question the solution or the approach. They have a mindset, 'This is what my senior leader said, so this is what I will do.' This mindset overrules any consideration of how much this misinformation or misguided direction will cost the organization in wasted resource hours, completion time, and progress, ultimately negatively impacting the bottom line. Recall when I referenced in the Purpose that I have witnessed entire departments be dissolved. Well, this is the type of situation that could result in the dissolution of a department because a transformation failed due to an issue rooted in the boss-subordinate dynamic. In said situations, who will be held accountable for the bad decision? In my experience, it is rarely the leader who made the bad call; it is usually the employees who are not empowered to speak up.

I can attest to personally experiencing this type of behavior from leaders I have worked with. I am still shocked when I encounter it. What's even more egregious is that I know every single leader from whom I have observed this type of behavior has undergone extensive leadership training to get to their level. It is almost as if what they are learning in leadership development is a theory, but they cannot apply the principles in practice. This is where TAAP™ comes into play. TAAP™ positions these leaders to empower themselves to transform their mindset and leadership style, aligning core values across the organization to pivot and meet market demands effectively.

Do you recall the assertion by Kotter and Forbes previously mentioned? As a recap, there is a 70% failure rate among businesses that attempt some form of change initiative or transformation. In 2021, a meta-analysis was conducted, which focuses on the financial data and reputations of corporations that have undergone a major transformation. The findings indicate that among these corporations, 78% of transformations failed. Of the 22% of successful organizations, it could be attributed to the level at which the companies engaged and shared a common focus with their employees. If you share a common focus with your employees, the commonality is likely not rooted in fear. These statistics indicate that over the past 25 years, organizations have gotten progressively worse at change initiatives and business transformations, even with the introduction of new tools, frameworks, and methodologies into the market. I assert that this is the time for a disruptive approach. It is time for TAAP™.

Let's consider these business transformations, which focus on a fundamental shift in how an organization conducts business. The catalyst for this transformation is typically aimed at addressing a complex business problem within the organization or an attempt to pivot to meet new market or technological demands, which presents a new set of complex business problems for the organization.

The harsh reality is that most failures are rooted in the dynamics of leadership and the mindset of the leaders themselves. I want to stress that I am not finger pointing finger or playing the blame game. Leaders are an asset to an organization and are vital in driving culture and ensuring organizational success. I am identifying the problem while at the same time presenting a solution. Historically, teams look to leaders to provide guidance to identify and solution the problem. But how can you look to a leader who may be on the hamster wheel themselves? How can we hold leaders accountable when a fear-based culture is at play?

The failed complex problem solutioning efforts I have participated in or witnessed could almost always be traced back to an organization with a fear-based, boss-subordinate culture. That said, as an industry, let's spend less time introducing new tools, frameworks, and methodologies and more time developing new approaches that normalize leaders using existing tools proven to successfully solution complex business problems. As a general rule: the focus should be on **people first, processes, and then tools.** Most business transformations focus on processes and tools and then people who are used as a vehicle to execute the solution. Let's shift to people first and start with our leaders!

CASE STUDY 7

The Impact of Fear-Based Leadership

In one of my most extreme experiences, I was assigned to be the project manager of a major business transformation. When I met with the sponsor to discuss their vision, I was informed that they had already developed an approach. In essence, this senior leader went beyond providing the vision and defined how their vision was to be delivered. I voiced concern that this approach would not be feasible given we had not assessed or defined key stakeholders. I was then informed that the stakeholders had already been identified, and that was the approach we would go with. Regardless of what I said, it was made clear that I was expected to use this approach.

100

Understanding the level of impact this would have on the organization, I voiced concerns given my internal knowledge and experience as a subject matter expert. I pointed out that I planned to use industry best practices to execute whatever vision and desired deliverables were provided. This would save time and ensure we had a clearly defined plan and allocated resources based on skill set and availability. The sponsor had a concern that people would be left out. I reassured the sponsor that all key stakeholders would play a role and participate in the tasks. I showed an example of a communication and strategy deployment plan we could use to track stakeholders and ensure everyone had an opportunity to participate. The sponsor was still adamant about moving forward with the no-plan plan.

I struggled to get a clear vision because the sponsor was more focused on starting the work without documenting a clear plan. I later learned that this individual had already discussed their plan with their leader, a high-ranking senior executive, and to backtrack would make them look bad. What was expected of me as the project manager was to be a coordinator and do what I was told. *But why would this leader not want to adjust their approach given the benefits I highlighted above?*

To garner support, I spoke with my direct leader, who stated they agreed with me but who was a lower-ranking leader and appeared to have less political power than the sponsor. As a result, they claimed they would address the concern but ultimately did nothing. Why would my leader not support me and voice our concerns? I attempted to rally leaders who were also on the team - all higher ranking than me. Those I spoke with agreed but would say nothing. Why would they not collectively voice their concern?

Everyone was given marching orders, and I prevented them from getting started because of my questions and concerns. Ironically, they wanted to start even though they knew the direction they were headed in would result in them marching right over the hill into a bottomless pit. The approach's validity and the work's value did not matter; they had a task to complete and would comply at all costs.

What I found most disturbing was that, as leaders, they must have known on some level that this behavior would ultimately lead to layoffs. There is a connection between failing to speak up and poor decision-making regarding employee stability. It is my hope that your awareness will motivate you to be more mindful of the immediate and long-term impact your decisions have not only on the organization but also on its employees.

Although the initiative failed, I didn't expect to be used as the scapegoat; despite this group awarding me a certificate and thanking me for doing an excellent job during the effort, I also participated in the hiring process for one of the leaders' selections of a new Director for their department. This person had praised me for my work and felt I could add value to selecting the best candidate for the position. I was delighted to hear during my weekly check-in with my direct leader shortly after the culmination of the initiative that the entire group reported to the Senior VP of the division that I was doing an excellent job. So, imagine my surprise when I received a negative evaluation a few weeks later. None of my hard work over the six months was recognized. I was genuinely shocked at the lengths this group would go to "get out of trouble." I was even more appalled at the passive people in the group who kept apologizing as if the attack on me could be resolved with an 'I am sorry, I thought you did a great job' or 'I wish we would have gone with your approach.' Of course, it was all said in private. No one spoke up or supported me publicly.

During my evaluation, my leader informed me that because I questioned a senior leader and attempted to get support from others on the team - regardless of whether they agreed that the direction was not right - I was wrong! He said to me, "You can't do that." I replied, "What do you mean? This sponsor ultimately publicly acknowledged that the approach was not working and tried to pivot to correct the bad call, but it was too late." He replied, "I agreed with you that it was the wrong call, but you can't say that to the sponsor or anyone else," Because I questioned the sponsor's approach and solicited feedback from other members (all senior to me), I supposedly made the group feel uncomfortable. Once the project was over, some reported no longer feeling comfortable working with me. As a result, I went from having one of the highest performance marks to being pummeled. The worst part was that I went from working at an organization I loved and gave 150% of my efforts to hating every day and struggling to smile or engage with my peers. I no longer trusted my leadership. I no longer respected any of them. This was my first dose of an organizational culture rooted in a toxic teacher-student dynamic.

The sponsor of this project was the perfect example of someone with the proper credentials but outdated experience. Or maybe the sponsor didn't have any experience. I couldn't discern which. The credentials, however, were remarkably similar to the ones I held, and I looked forward to working with this person because of this. Two of their credentials were industry-recognized—a testament to someone who has the certifications but lacks the skills. I firmly believe certifications are the stepping stone to a lifelong journey and commitment to remain a subject matter expert. You never stop learning, just as you never stop solutioning. You are responsible for applying the knowledge you learn and engaging with like-minded professionals to ensure you are doing so correctly. On paper, this leader outranked me, but they did not have the expertise necessary to ensure a successful initiative, nor did they have the integrity to own their part in the failure of the transition.

In my 20 years of working across multiple industries, I have never experienced anything remotely close to this level of toxicity. This entire group of leaders exhibited conflict-avoidant behavior to prevent being reprimanded by their boss and ostracized by their peers. I found the private apologies and request to work with them more insulting and disgusting than the group's attack.

⁂

III.

The reality is when you don't speak up and address problems immediately, they can fester, and small problems become larger problems, and larger problems morph into complex problems. This leads to the misuse of time and effort and missed opportunities to assess a reliable plan, thus impacting the efficiency of the organization's ecosystem and ultimately, the bottom line. These ripple effects occur simply because an individual, or sometimes a group of leaders, decide to ignore an issue, disempower staff, and choose not to pivot in their approach to a solution.

When organizations do not effectively address complex business problems within their operational ecosystem, specifically related to poor or non-existent processes and technologies, they will struggle to meet their market's ever-changing, ever-evolving demands. This is a big deal because they will experience a decline in their financial performance. When such organizations are unsuccessful in reversing this trend, typically through a change initiative or business transformation, usually within a few quarters, they will need to move towards strategically restructuring and eliminating wastes that impact the bottom line. This is a fancy way of saying, 'cutting the cost of labor' or 'layoffs'!

The reality is inefficient organizations lay people off. I am not saying that *only* inefficient organizations lay people off. I am saying inefficient organizations will ultimately lay people off. The less efficient an organization is, the more likely you will see layoffs. As a leader, should you bear any responsibility for your organization's ecosystems? What about operational efficiency within that ecosystem? When faced with complex business problems, if you suppress subject matter experts from delivering what is necessary because it is not what you prefer, you become part of the problem. You're not acting in the best interest of the organization or the employees when you prioritize protecting yourself, being dutiful, or mitigating your fears. Should you be held accountable? If this describes you as a leader, understand that, ultimately, both the employees and the organization will eventually pay the price.

By adopting the TAAP™ approach, organizations cultivate a culture of self-empowerment driven by leaders who encourage open dialogue and empower their teams to voice concerns. With leader's adept at pivoting to address market and technological shifts proactively, the need for major business transformations diminishes, fostering stability and adaptability.

IV.

If there is one thing I can stress, it is that effective leadership does not work in theory - it thrives in *practice*. Practice requires skilled and experienced leaders who can reinterpret and apply what they have learned to their environment. They embrace continuous learning and are empowered to challenge approaches, make decisions, and drive change fearlessly. As a leader, you will never have all the answers. Your role is to provide resources and guidance to those subject matter experts who specialize in executing solutions and delivering value. This type of leader can successfully lead the effort for complex problem solutioning.

The best advice I could give any leader is to get comfortable approaching your career as a lifelong journey. You are responsible for defining what should be accomplished in each role you hold. You set the vision. Your staff are the subject matter experts who define *how* to execute and achieve your vision. You are not standing on the sidelines, but you are not calling the shots either. There is a balance. Without balance and the respect and trust of your subject matter experts and team, you will fail. Your role is to provide guidance, support, and resources where appropriate. Steve Jobs said it best: "It doesn't make sense to hire smart people and tell them what to do; we hire smart people so they can tell us what to do." As a leader, you may be unable to fix a teacher-student dynamic in your organization's culture single-handedly. Still, you can effect change by choosing a different path of leadership. Start by embracing TAAP™ to "be the leader you wish you had." – Simon Sinek.

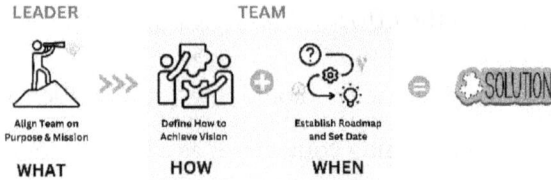

LEADER · TEAM

Align Team on Purpose & Mission — Define How to Achieve Vision — Establish Roadmap and Set Date

WHAT · HOW · WHEN

SOLUTION

Unless you are a natural-born leader, which is rare, it does not matter how many degrees, courses, trainings, or books on leadership development you consume. Suppose you do not commit to understanding your personality characteristics and traits that dictate how you perceive and respond to situations in your environment. In that case, your effectiveness as a leader, especially when it comes to solutioning complex business problems, will be fruitless. Complex business problems don't just appear; they are usually the result of a hodgepodge of factors, including the teacher-student dynamic in an organization's culture, poor leadership, weak or non-existent processes and technologies, internal politics, employee apathy, and difficulty adjusting to changes within the market and technology.

If you don't understand your personality as a leader or have confidence in your employees' abilities, your chances of successful complex business solutioning are slim. Think about it this way: if you have a culture built on a foundation of adaptability and continuous improvement where employees are empowered to question, call out issues, and act, how long do you think a problem will fester or, even worse, experience what I experienced in Case Study 7? The probability of a complex business problem going unnoticed in this type of environment would be highly unlikely. Unless it is associated with market changes or technological advancements, I argue that the odds of morphing from a simple problem to a complex one will be slim to none because employees would be empowered to speak up and act! This may sound too good to be true, but it isn't. It requires leaders who are bold and willing to take the time to plan a solution.

Authentic leadership development is a personal journey. Take advantage of the tools available, but at the end of the day, effective leaders are not created out of training courses, seminars, or a really good book. I believe effective leaders evolve through a personal commitment of 80% continued self-development and empowerment and 20% education.

PART TWO

Navigate Social Constructs

ARE YOU THE PUZZLE PIECE THAT DOESN'T FIT?

I.

If you have been the victim of poor decision-making by your leadership or organization's politics, you likely felt powerless, frustrated, angry, or hopeless. You possibly even questioned your competency. Hopefully, you chose your field because you're passionate about it and want to learn new skills from more experienced people. I have personally witnessed others struggle with letting go, especially if they see the potential, know they have an idea of how to make things better or have a solution to a problem. Don't allow a single person to derail you from developing your skills or accomplishing your true purpose. As someone who has had to accept a hard dose of reality about my leaders and the fact that they had no interest in aligning their behaviors and decisions with the organization's core values, I now understand I was a puzzle piece that did not fit. Working in this environment is not sustainable; it's mentally draining. And life is too short. Move on. Find an organization whose core values and purpose align with your personal core values and purpose. Or better yet, create your own organization or write a book! ☺

II.

If you are frustrated because your leadership is constantly choosing to do what's easy over what's right, ask yourself: Am I in the right place? Do I truly belong here? Is it an environment conducive to my growth, or does it prioritize compliance over individual expression? Additionally, consider whether the leadership's actions reflect the organization's core values and ensure the organization's culture resonates with your personal core values. The more you understand your personal core values and what you would like to work on to add value outside your desired salary, the more likely you will find an organization that aligns with your goals.

I have been in positions where I believed that if I were the example of striving toward excellence, the leaders would see the benefits. As a result, we would improve the environment as a team. Can these types of transformations happen from the bottom up? Yes, they can, but it takes a lot of work. The reality is you may be viewed as a threat if you can't get other employees to support you; more than likely, it is because they are operating out of the same 'fear-based' culture as their leaders. So, you will be a target and the risks are high. You could lose your job. Even worse, depending on your industry, a twisted narrative could spread, affecting opportunities for future employment. You have a decision to make. You can try to transform the culture or move on and find a place where you belong. Whatever your decision, make sure that it is something that brings you joy. I always tell my clients and mentees to remember that they are a number on a spreadsheet at the end of the day. And if your number doesn't line up with the organization's bottom line, you will be cut.

As an employee, you need to look at employment like the employer. When the relationship is no longer mutually beneficial, and you are spending more time trying to help improve the culture or convince leadership to change while also being required to complete work you are not paid for, the numbers no longer add up. You are effectively giving more than agreed. The organization is no longer adding value to your bottom line, and it may be time for renegotiation or a self-cut.

Any efforts to execute complex business problem solutioning in environments with a teacher-student mindset, a culture of fear-based leadership, a lack of leadership support, or internal politics will likely be fruitless. Complex problem-solutioning requires employees who are empowered to do their jobs. They define the problem based on data, not leadership demands. They are bold. They address issues head-on and make decisions based on genuine collaborative discussions. I understand that no organization is perfect, but these types of cultures rooted in fear and toxic work environments don't align with what is necessary to successfully solution complex problems, simply because the focus is not on what's in the best interest of the organization, but what is in the best interest of individuals who are either avoiding conflict or are trying to climb the corporate ladder.

ESCAPE THE HAMSTER WHEEL THROUGH CULTURAL TRANSFORMATION

I.

As painful as it is to admit, I have been on the proverbial hamster wheel. There have been times in my career when I have found myself running so hard that I barely ate or slept, all for the greater good, sacrificing my needs and mental health in the process. I believed if I slowed down, I would lose control and go flying off into the abyss. Everything was lost.

As a leader, a need for accolades does not drive me to achieve success. I am motivated by a conscious fear of massive failure driven by a desire to deliver excellence. Professionally, when working on a problem, I aim to ensure I don't fail. In the past, I would start what should be a marathon off with a powerful sprint. Instead of slowing down and pacing myself, I ran harder and harder until I was either forced to slow down from sheer exhaustion or I outpaced those around me and had to wait for them to catch up. Other times, I simply failed. And boy, when I failed, I failed miserably. If you are anything like me, you don't take failure well. As an Agilest, I am okay with incremental failure; I understand this will get me to my goal. But complete failure of an effort takes a mental and emotional toll, and I would need time to recuperate and reflect. Surprisingly, when things calmed down, and I processed what happened, there was always this massive sense of relief because I escaped the hamster wheel! But did I? How many times have you been through a similar experience, and like me, you jumped right back on the hamster wheel only to start the cycle again?

I realized I did this because I believed this was the only way to maintain control. It was also a great adrenaline rush to push and test the limits of my abilities. In situations where you're always working and feel you have control, know that you don't. Your environment dictates your behavior, goals, decisions, and daily tasks. In essence, your environment controls you. You become a professional taskmaster. You are so focused on meeting the needs of the existing environment that you are less effective and inefficient. You are often unaware of the problems brewing in the background because you've developed tunnel vision. You don't have the awareness or usually the ability to leverage the tools and resources in your environment to make effective decisions or efficiently plan consciously.

II.

Tesla entered the automotive market in 2011, and less than a decade later, the organization's presence forced traditional automakers to rethink their business models, invest in innovative technologies, and shift towards more sustainable transportation options. Tesla has, in a brief period, disrupted a virtually impenetrable industry. Tesla's story is a perfect example of what Disruptive Innovation means. **Disruptive Innovation** is a term coined by Clayton Christensen in the early 1990s to describe the impact when a new business or product is introduced to the market and upends significant players or even goes as far as transforming an entire industry.

Being disruptive in business means bringing a literal jolt to the marketplace; it introduces innovative alternative products and ultimately changes the way business is conducted. Tesla was both disruptive and innovative. Think about it.

Fifteen years ago, if someone had said that Ford's American Classic Mustang - known for its powerful engine and horsepower - would run on a battery, would you believe them? Now that's Disruptive Innovation!

While we are making tremendous strides across industries, we also face significant challenges. We live in an era where terms like "quiet quitting" and "the great resignation" are becoming the norm. In 2023, 2,500 plus organizations announced major layoffs, resulting in over six million people losing their jobs in the USA. Many of these organizations and employees feared a looming recession and were operating in survival mode. They were trying to minimize the impact of their current problems by getting ahead to lessen the impact of future problems.

Not all disruptive innovations have as big of an impact as Tesla has on the automotive industry, but innovation is occurring across industries every day. It is the catalyst for evolution in the marketplace, which is exciting but has a downside. As industries evolve, technologies become more advanced, and organizational operations and processes risk becoming unstable due to the inability to adapt to the necessary changes rapidly. With innovation, problems become more complex. The question is, are businesses equipped with the skills to address the increased complexities of their problems?

III.

Organizations that do well during phases of innovation are those whose culture aligns with their core values and mission. Their culture is rooted in a continuous improvement mindset, and they can quickly adapt to change. They have, in many ways, become Agile. But what about the employees? If an industry is changing and the organization is agile enough to adapt, it will also require agile employees, right? Are organizations ensuring their employees embody the intended culture and have the skills to adapt to this evolving agile environment?

If we look at the trend in messaging of 2023's major corporations when they laid people off, it is associated with economic downturn, restructuring within organizations, automation, and technical advancements. These changes led to the need for an adjustment in job roles and a reduction of work force to meet the shift in market demands. What is leadership consistently doing to ensure that as the market shifts and demands of the organization are changing their current employees have the skills to stay ahead of the curve? Nothing.

To give you an idea of the rate at which the market is changing, technology is advancing, and the challenges companies face with remaining competitive, Elon Musk announced a 10% cut to his global workforce while I made final edits on this chapter! He said that the electric vehicle market has grown so rapidly that it has resulted in a duplication of some roles within Tesla. He also noted that the average tenure of senior-level executives at Tesla is ten years, which has slowed innovation. He posited that by eliminating these roles, "Tesla becomes more lean, innovative, and hungry for the next growth phase." His belief is that Tesla's layoffs will position the company to operate efficiently and meet ever-evolving market demands.

As you can imagine, like Thor, the mighty God of Thunder, with his sledgehammer in tow (I am in no way referring to Elon Musk as a God), a memo was sent out close to midnight on Sunday the 14th of April 2024 to eliminate 10%

of Tesla's global workforce which amounts to approximately 14,000 people who relied on this company for their livelihood, yet with the push of a button their roles were immediately dissolved with the following words, *"Effective now, you will not need to perform any further work and therefore will no longer have access to Tesla systems and physical locations."* As an employee, in reality, you are a mere figure on a spreadsheet, and if your role fails to add value to the organization's bottom line, it is eliminated, and you are dismissed. These employees found themselves on the chopping block when their roles resulted in duplicate expenses on Tesla's balance sheet. It is in moments like this that the necessity of the TAAP™ approach becomes abundantly clear.

The norm in American business culture is to prioritize the customer first, the company, and then the employee. Consider the memo from Elon Musk, and you are a Tesla employee preparing for work on Monday. What if you do not check your email Sunday night? You will either show up to work or log in to your computer on Monday only to find you are locked out of the company system or your badge to enter the parking lot, let alone the building no longer works. Consider there are mandated laws in states such as California under the WARN notice, which requires at least 60 days advanced notice of an upcoming layoff, but not all states have this requirement.

An employee embodies the essence of the organization, yet is often regarded as disposable, like interchangeable parts in a machine. Their worth is reduced to mere functionality, they're replaced at a whim, overlooking the unique value each brings to the whole.

Until this mindset and behavior changes, we will continue to have cycles of massive layoffs. If you are a leader faced with a similar issue as Elon Musk, I challenge you to, instead of viewing employees as expenses on a spreadsheet, consider them as human beings with a set of skills your company has invested in and helped develop during their tenure with your organization. This shift in mindset will affect decisions related to massive layoffs.

Consider, for example, each corporate employee entering an organization has, at minimum, a set of five technical skills related to their current role, which can be directly attributed to adding to a company's bottom line. Within 2 years, the employee has mastered the existing skills, but through a Transformative Agile™ Leadership style and purposeful disruption, the employee can develop the necessary new skills to meet the technological demands and advancements of the market. A Transformative Agile™ company is ever-evolving, and the odds of a duplication of roles are highly unlikely due to the self-evolving nature of its teams and the purposefully disruptive mindset of its leadership.

Approximately 14,000 people lost their livelihoods — their employment — because Tesla, which entered the market in 2010 as a disruptor and innovator in the automotive industry, found itself 14 years later struggling to keep competitors at bay. While Musk attributes the company's inefficiencies to the tenure of his leadership, I believe that the root cause of the issue lies not in the length of time Tesla's leadership has been in place but rather in their mindset and leadership style during their tenure.

As a leader, I hope that as you transform your mindset, you embrace TAAP™ and a Transformative Agile™ leadership style, you build self-evolving and self-empowered teams in which you prioritize the employee first, the company, and then the customer. Controversial, yes, I know! Hear me out: imagine a sports team preparing for a championship game. Traditionally, the focus has been on strategies to win the game at any cost, often neglecting the physical and mental well-being of the players. There's pressure to please the fans and prioritize their demands. This approach mirrors the customer-centric model in business. However, a new coach arrives with a different approach. Instead of solely prioritizing victory (the organization's bottom line) or satisfying the fans (the customer), the coach emphasizes the health, morale, and development of each player (the employee). As a result, the team performs better on the field and fosters a supportive and cohesive environment where everyone thrives. Similarly, by prioritizing the employee first, the company can build a solid foundation for success, leading to sustainable growth and a thriving work culture.

Let us be honest: the heart of any business is its employees, yet we are inundated with the slogan "customer first" and often hear about the importance of services or products to ensure customer satisfaction, but what about the employees? They are the gears that keep the machinery running smoothly. Without them, even the most cutting-edge products or stellar customer service strategies would falter. Think about it. Employees bring the products or services to life by interacting directly with customers to understand their needs and ensure they are met. And let's not forget the employees' dedication, skills, and creativity, which drive an organization's growth. So, when we talk about prioritizing the employee first, it's not just a nice sentiment; it's a strategic necessity. Without happy and motivated employees, the entire operation would grind to a halt, regardless of the greatness of the products or services, the number of customers, or the leadership skill level. Yes, admittedly, employees are replaceable, but the continuous churn of new employees disrupts an organization's culture. If you make the employees your priority, they will make your customers theirs! This is the power of an employee-centric approach.

Embrace a shift in perspective. It's time to purposefully disrupt the traditional view of employees within the industry. While acknowledging the longstanding debate around this topic, we must ask: why not adopt a truly employee-centric approach that prioritizes a balance of high customer value? Let's look at a company that leveraged its core values to drive its culture and placed its employees first.

CASE STUDY 8

Driving Culture Through Core Values

Zappos, an online shoe retailer known for being an employee-centric company with a strong emphasis on culture, embarked on an innovative journey to shape its organizational structure in 2010. Spearheaded by the late CEO Tony Hsieh and a workforce of approximately 1500 employees, the company dedicated a year to meticulously crafting its first core values ten years after its founding and committed to them afterward. Hsieh said, "We wanted a list of committable core values that we were willing to hire and fire on. If we weren't willing to do that, then they weren't really 'values.'"

This collaborative effort culminated in the establishment of ten core values, each representing the ethical compass and dedication of Zappos' workforce:

1. Deliver the Wow Through Service
2. Embrace and Drive Change
3. Create Fun and A Little Weirdness
4. Be Adventurous, Creative, and Open-Minded
5. Pursue Growth and Learning
6. Build Open and Honest Relationships with Communication
7. Build a Positive Team and Family Spirit
8. Do More with Less
9. Be Passionate and Determined
10. Be Humble

The company provided employees with color-coded badges representing each of the ten core values to ensure their core values were not lost in translation or forgotten after employee onboarding. Employees selected a badge that corresponded to the value they committed to uphold. Notably, following its acquisition by Amazon, Hsieh orchestrated measures to safeguard Zappos' distinctive culture from assimilation into Amazon's culture. As the company evolved, it embarked on a radical transformation, dissolving all managerial positions and favoring a Holarctic model in 2013. Groundbreaking as it was, this transition modeled what innovation looked like.

This bold move decentralized decision-making authority and redistributed responsibilities across self-organizing teams termed "circles." The overarching objective was to empower employees with the autonomy and adaptability to make decisions aligned with the company's purpose, culture, and budgetary constraints. As of 2024, while Zappos maintains its circle structure, it is gradually reverting certain facets of its operations to a more conventional corporate model.

The phrase encapsulates a common mindset at Zappos: 'The only thing constant at Zappos is change.' This mantra continues to permeate the company's core values. This shift does not signify a failure despite a semi-transition back to a traditional model. Instead, it exemplifies the company's proactive approach to questioning norms and implementing transformative solutions that purposefully disrupt the status quo. This underscores Zappo's unwavering commitment to evolving while staying true to its core values and employee-centric culture.

IV.

Innovation can be a double-edged sword. On the one hand, the potential for advancement is fantastic, but organizations and employees must take responsibility and not just expect to reap the benefits of innovation. They need to make sure they adapt, stay ahead of the curve, and develop the skills to address the complex business problems that come with innovation. I can't think of anything worse than an organization with issues that can't be resolved because leadership is behind the curve, and employees do not have the skill sets to address them.

As Newsweek projected, massive layoffs will affect over half of U.S. organizations in 2024. If there was ever a time to be disruptive with a purpose, it is now. Innovation is needed to derail what is becoming a norm in our economy. If massive layoffs become the norm, how will this affect our society?

What I find more infuriating than the number of layoffs that have occurred and will occur is the many employees who buy into the strategic messaging that organizations shell out. "You are valued." "You are important." "We will pay for your health insurance." "We will give you a fair bonus." "We will pay you a fair wage." "We will pay for your education and certifications if you desire to advance your learning." "This is a safe place." "We support you." The reality is most of these actions are required by law, and the real motivation is for the organization to remain competitive to get you in the door and keep you there until you are no longer needed. Remember, the priority is the customer → organization, → employee. Nothing is more heartbreaking than seeing an employee who has dedicated their life and sacrificed family time, happiness, and health because they trusted and believed in their organization. Only one day, they show up to work ready to continue giving their all and be informed that they are no longer a part of the organization.

I have been laid off twice in my career. The first time I was laid off, I was the employee who believed I was an asset to the organization because my job was to find inefficiencies and make improvements. Right before I was laid off, I and a colleague discovered a significant amount of fraud via the misuse of employee credit cards. In collaboration with HR, Accounting, Finance, IT, and corporate, we implemented a new credit card system at no cost to the organization. I was fortunate to negotiate with the bank and convince them to provide this service for free. The benefits of cost savings and eliminating the misappropriation of funds were immediate, yet I was still let go. Ironically, I swore to never work for an organization again. I began to work as a consultant and independent contractor for several years until COVID hit. I decided to accept a position at another organization, where I was laid off again after three years of employment. The difference between the two layoffs was that I was devastated and unprepared financially and emotionally for the first time. The second time, I knew I would be laid off at least eight months in advance. *Lay me off once, and I don't see it coming; shame on you. Lay me off twice, and I don't see it coming; shame on me!*

When I accepted the last position, I showed up every day with the expectation that at any moment, it could be my last. In my mind, I had long-term temporary employment. I say this to you because as we move through this process of being disruptive, it requires a level of commitment that will feel as if it is permanent. Complex problem solutioning and being disruptive with a purpose should be treated as permanent within the organization. You, as an employee, are not. Be dedicated. Give it your all. But also, be okay with detaching yourself enough, so it is easy to walk away at any time. Leaders, this section applies to you as you are also an employee of an organization.

V.

When you think of the flows of communication pathways, most major organizations have departments that consistently assess the market and have a good idea of potential shifts. Leadership uses this information to protect and reposition strategically to ensure the organization can survive market changes. At this stage, I have yet to see anyone assess whether their employees have the skills to ride the wave with the organization. The current approach is a mindset like spring cleaning: out with the old to make way with the new.

Typically, organizations with unstable operations and processes operate in quiet chaos, cross-functional confusion, silos, and pervasive wasted resource time and effort. This is their norm. In these types of environments, not only are the employees suffering from **the Hamster Wheel Effect**™, but you will find the organization's day-to-day operations are also deeply embedded and operate on a highly complex hamster wheel, typically spinning so fast you don't know it's there. In a sense, it is the most efficient and undetectable form of chaos you'll experience. The organization is essentially operating with tunneled-visioned leaders and employees. Depending on its level of maturity, if you observe this type of organization from the outside looking in, everything may appear okay. But when you ask probing questions, you will find significant problems that must be addressed.

There is nothing more frustrating than the Hamster Wheel Effect™. Leadership typically has a mindset of 'no time for planning or slowing down' to assess the root cause of complex business problems, let alone establish processes to prevent complex business problems from developing. Solutions are implemented based on a consensus of assumptions; usually, the loudest voice with the most political prowess in the group wins. The cycle continues: wasted resource efforts and time, quiet quitting, the great resignation, and failed initiative after failed initiative. Leadership and employees develop the mindset that their problems are impossible to solution, so they remain in survival mode.

Failure is not fun. If nothing disrupts a consistent pattern of failure, it will become the norm and affect the organization's morale. Failing to learn how to stay ahead of the innovation curve, build skills, and foster an adaptive culture that embraces consistent change to address complex business problems will inevitably force an organization and its employees on a problem-solutioning hamster wheel. This will only end when the organization is bought out or permanently closes its doors. That's a massive failure.

Recognizing the Hamster Wheel Effect™ begins with first identifying if you and your employees are operating on a hamster wheel. Ask yourself the following questions. **As an employee, I have said or heard a colleague say this phrase or similar phrase, such as:**

1. 'Well, at least we have…'
2. 'I am just grateful we at least have something in place…'

133

3. 'Well, it could be worse…"

4. "I guess we'll just have to deal with it,"

5. "Isn't this just how things have always been?"

6. "I wish someone would address this issue, but it's probably not going to happen."

7. "I'm just here to do my job and collect my paycheck."

Or, as a leader, you or a colleague in a leadership position have expressed the following or similar sentiment:

1. 'There's nothing I/we can do…,'

2. 'I can't, or we can't…,'

3. 'It's just the way things are….'

4. 'Yes, I know this is a problem, but it is not a hill worth dying on…'

5. 'I knew this wouldn't work, but getting people to listen wasn't worth the fight.'

6. "We've tried to address this before, but it never goes anywhere."

7. "I'm not sure if anyone would support changing this…"

8. "The problem isn't a priority right now."

9. "It is not my responsibility to fix this."

These comments indicate that you and your organization may suffer from the Hamster Wheel Effect™. Your organization's culture is not built on aligned core values or a continuous improvement mindset. People are okay with conforming to the status quo and are afraid to rock the boat. In addition, your operations and processes are unstable; it is a true 'good is good enough' environment with survivors, not thrivers. In situations such as this, it would behoove leadership to act immediately. Without proper operational stability, leadership and employees eventually become apathetic, less engaged, and less apt to identify problems, let alone initiate effective improvement efforts. Failing to act allows the vicious cycle of the Hamster Wheel Effect™ to continue.

VI.

To escape the hamster wheel as a leader or employee, like Tesla when it was first introduced to the marketplace, you must be a disruptor! Instead of an industry, you will disrupt your organization's operations, rules of engagement, and how it solutions complex business problems. You will disrupt your mindset. You will transform yourself and the tunnel-visioned taskmasters into proactive problem solutioners who embody a culture of continuous improvement and a commitment to sustainability.

As a leader, you will send a jolt through your operations to improve efficiency and effectiveness and ultimately change how you do business. This task is not easy, but it is possible with the right mindset, support, and tools. This transformation will occur over time. It took Tesla 10 years to become a norm and change the culture of the auto industry. I am not saying it will take you or your organization ten years, but you will need patience, a thirst for new knowledge, dedication, perseverance, and buy-in.

CASE STUDY 9

Purposeful Disruption: The 30-Year Journey of India's Forest Man

Jadav Payeng, known as India's Forest Man, is a testament to the power of purposeful disruption and non-conformity in environmental conservation. Over a span of three decades, Payeng single-handedly transformed a barren sandbar into a thriving forest ecosystem, defying conventional norms and inspiring a global movement toward ecological restoration. He was born and raised in the northeastern state of Assam, India, and saw firsthand the devastating effects of deforestation on the once-lush landscapes of his homeland. Determined to make a difference, he embarked on a remarkable journey that would change the course of environmental conservation in his region.

In the early 1980s, Payeng began planting a few bamboo saplings on a desolate sandbar along the Brahmaputra River. Despite facing skepticism and ridicule from his community, he remained steadfast in his commitment to revitalizing the barren land. Undeterred by the enormity of the task, he devoted himself to tending to the tiny saplings every day. Over time, his efforts bore fruit and transformed into a lush green forest teeming with diverse flora and fauna.

Through his innovative approach to afforestation and unwavering determination, Payeng defied conventional wisdom and achieved what people thought was impossible! He demonstrated that individual action, fueled by passion and purpose, could catalyze transformative change on a monumental scale. Today, Payeng's forest, known as the Molai Forest or "Molai Woods," spans over 1,360 acres and serves as a vital habitat for countless species of plants and animals. His pioneering efforts have restored biodiversity and mitigated soil erosion, protected local communities from floods, and sequestered significant amounts of carbon dioxide from the atmosphere.

If one man can afforest over 1,360 acres, what can we, together, achieve to solution complex business problems within our organizations and beyond? By planting this seed of inspiration, I urge you to approach complex problems with renewed vigor, refusing to accept a blind eye or inept solutions. Instead, think outside the box as a leader and leverage Transformative Agile™ and purposeful disruption to drive meaningful change.

SOCIAL CONSTRUCTS SHAPE BEHAVIOR

I.

There's often a misconception surrounding disruptors - they're perceived as troublemakers. However, it's vital to strike a balance between disruption and conformity, not only in business but also in broader societal contexts. Imagine a world where every idea is challenged merely for the sake of challenging or where people always agree to avoid conflict. In such a world, we would never progress. Recognize that disruptors aren't disruptive for the sake of disrupting or even to cause trouble; they genuinely believe there is an opportunity to improve things. I would argue India's Forest Man in Case Study 9 exemplifies a leader committed to purposeful disruption.

Imagine a world where everyone simply conformed to group behavior without question. Where would we find ourselves? I'd likely be enslaved. This may sound far-fetched, but it holds truth. Under the umbrella of social constructs, disruption, and conformity reside, shaping not only individual actions but also entire organizations and societies, potentially leading to the loss of personal freedom and autonomy. Social rules influence us and define constructs based on our interactions and perceptions. These constructs dictate which norms we adhere to and which ones we reject. They are the rules and ideas defined and upheld by the group. It is within the group that social standards, behaviors, and beliefs are established. For any group, these constructs define their reality, influencing how they perceive and respond to change, their performance, and ultimately their success. In this context, disruptive leaders exhibit the behavioral output of a specific social construct known as **informational internalization**, a concept we will explore further in this chapter.

Reflecting on the incident with my direct leader and the leadership group in Case Study 7, I realized that the group expected me to conform and accept the existing social constructs. These were unwritten and unspoken but very real. They defined the rules of engagement between subordinates and leaders. I chose not to comply, so I was a threat to the group and received consequences for my non-compliance. In fact, within this group, these constructs were also based on levels of role and political power.

Given I did not comply, and honestly if given the chance to do it again, I still would not comply, I believed in what I was doing. I knew from experience and established industry best practices that the current approach would not work. I stayed true to my core values: Accountability, Ethical Integrity, Communication and Clarity, Collaboration, Self-Awareness and Personal-Growth, and Empowerment and Excellence.

Although I did not recognize it then, I was an outsider to the group. I was attempting to disrupt social constructs to deliver what I believed to be excellence and value-adding. However, in the end, I was the enemy, which resulted in the group, making a collective decision to neutralize my ability to influence or continue to work on the initiative.

A complex business problem can be likened to a virus in an organization's day-to-day operations, weaving its way through processes. Some viruses are simple and pose minimal threats, while others are complex and pose significant threats. A disruptor's role is like a scientist trying to find a cure to combat the virus. They must identify and isolate the virus(es) that pose a threat and methodically develop a cure to neutralize the threat. If successful, day-to-day operations, like the immune system, are healthy, remain healthy, and grow stronger over time. If not, like the virus, a problem will fight back and exhibit a level of sophistication where symptoms disguise themselves as the problem or come back stronger, adapting after each attack. If not observant, the disruptor, like the scientist, will end up on a dead-end cycle of problem solutioning while the organization's operations, like the immune system, are weakened to incapacitation and even death.

Consider the number of iterations and trials it takes before a scientist produces a cure and your body starts producing healthy cells that can kill a virus. It is no different in disruptive problem solutioning™. This is why you must use proven approaches, frameworks, and methodologies to get to the root of the problem and be free of distractions from deceptive symptoms to ensure healthy processes and efficient operations are in place. Once you achieve this, are you okay? No. Constant monitoring is required to keep you healthy and hopefully develop a stronger immune system to continue staving off past viruses and any future ones. It will require sustainment and continuous improvements to ensure the complex business problem does not return. Understanding your organization's culture and social constructs is critical to ensuring you can solution existing complex business problems and prevent future ones.

There is also a cultural aspect as to why I am committed to and believe in the power of disruption. As a woman of African descent, I was raised to speak up when something is wrong because history has shown us that if no one says anything or stands against what's unfair or unjust, unthinkable things can happen. Think about the atrocities that have occurred because large groups of people accepted what was happening. This is not to ignore the fact that large groups of people, including their leaders and those with power within the group, believed in what they were doing. The key question is how many within this group complied simply because they wanted to be accepted, saw the benefits of complying, or were afraid? The two historical events that come to mind are the Chattel Enslavement of humans of African descent across the world and the Holocaust.

If my analogies make you uncomfortable, it is okay. I expect that they should, especially if you are not a person of African or Jewish descent. What type of conformity do you lean towards? Do you believe that there is a valid excuse for the atrocities that have occurred, or would you rather not discuss or think of things that make you uncomfortable? Whichever the reason, I suggest you push through your discomfort because ignoring it makes you susceptible to ignoring any future atrocities that may take place. If you are experiencing discomfort, it may be because these analogies touch on sensitive topics related to historical oppression and discrimination, which can evoke strong emotions and reactions. To alleviate your discomfort, you could approach the topics with an open mind, seek out diverse perspectives, and reflect on your own biases and privileges, which can contribute to personal growth and greater empathy towards other experiences.

I intend to help you understand that no matter whether it is a business problem or a societal problem, not speaking up and ignoring problems will allow them to fester, and the consequences are often something that the human mind, in hindsight, cannot fathom why it occurred in the first place. This is crucial because business problems can escalate into societal issues. Take, for example, the correlation between increased layoffs and the growing homelessness crisis nationwide. The homeless crisis across the country is known as a wicked problem – a complex societal issue that defies easy solutions and impacts multiple facets of society, not just those unhoused.

In 2020, an economist at Columbia University predicted that the number of layoffs sparked by the pandemic and statewide lockdowns is directly correlated to the expected increase of homelessness by 45%. This is approximately

250,000 people left unhoused because of losing their primary source of income. The Bureau of Labor Statistics (BLS) reported that in 2023, there was a total of 15.4 million Americans who had experienced a layoff. Forbes reported that 78% of Americans live paycheck to paycheck, and more than three-quarters struggle to save or invest after paying their monthly expenses. Being an employee is high risk and stressful; it is estimated that 48% of employees have layoff anxiety, and rightfully so, with 40% of Americans having been laid off or terminated from a job at least once. It takes an average of three to six months for an employee to find a new job, while severance packages cover an average of less than three months of expenses. The cost of living is likely not covered by unemployment; for example, in California, the maximum unemployment is 1800 dollars a month, whereas the average cost of living, according to sofi.com, is $4,423 a month. The stark reality is except for a small percentage of industries, a significant portion of people you encounter are likely living paycheck to paycheck and may face the prospect of being laid off.

As a leader, envision the above figures representing your employees, colleagues, or even yourself, facing the possibility of a layoff. Now that you understand the direct correlation between inefficient organizations and layoffs, coupled with the staggering 45% increase in homelessness attributed to such layoffs, how does this newfound awareness affect you? Do you acknowledge your responsibility for the decisions that directly correlate to inefficiencies in your organization, knowing that inefficient organizations lay people off?

Consider the grim reality: It is highly likely that some of your employees are living paycheck to paycheck and may face a layoff. Also, festering issues typically morph into complex business problems impacting operational efficiencies; it's imperative to reflect on the statements outlined in Chapter Five to determine whether you or your organization is stuck in a repetitive cycle or ineffective action - the Hamster Wheel Effect™. Let these statements serve as a guide as you contemplate your response. I hope that through the progression of this book, you've begun the mental groundwork necessary to accept accountability, take decisive action to empower yourself, and embrace TAAP™.

Empowered leaders and employees are disruptive. Their employees are empowered to speak up to prevent simple problems from morphing into complex ones. They speak up when decisions conflict with the company's core values. They speak up when decisions are not in the best interest of the collective whole and the organization. Organizations that embrace purposeful disruption operate more efficiently because they empower leaders and their employees to think holistically and do not allocate people (resources) to areas that will likely fail in the long term.

II.

If it weren't for the early disruptors, also known as abolitionists of the late 1700s until the abolitionist movement gained momentum in the 1830s, I would not be here writing this book! The length of time America actively practiced chattel slavery is longer than the length of time people of African descent were legally recognized no longer as property. The enslavement in America lasted approximately 246 years and ended only 158 years ago. This does not consider the continued fight for civil rights due to unwritten social constructs rooted in beliefs of inferiority and racial stereotypes of people of African descent. To provide even more context, it took at least 130 years for the abolitionist movement to catch on. That's 130 years for the collective group to speak up and gain enough power to not only say this is wrong but trigger a tipping point. In this time period, a group of human beings (e.g., families, men, women, and children) were legally brutalized because they were the physical property of another human being.

Whether in my personal or professional life, I am committed to remaining a disruptor because I understand the depths to which blind conformity can go, both personally and professionally. If it weren't for the unknown disruptors in the 1700s to the infamous ones of the 1800s, like Harriet Tubman, Nat Turner, William Loyd Garrison, and so many more, I would more than likely not exist due to the sheer brutality and treatment of my people during this era. Or I may have been born enslaved, not knowing how to read and certainly not writing about solutioning complex business problems.

That said, you can see why someone with my cultural background is uncomfortable complying with team-defined social constructs that I know are not right. Or quietly accepting the unjust reprimand in Case Study 2, which was layered with a misogynistic stereotype to incite fear and get me to conform to an approach that the entire group knew was wrong.

Now consider my additional layer of understanding: poor leadership decisions and disempowered staff contribute to squandered resources, perpetuating failed efforts that directly correlate to organizational layoffs and increased homelessness. Given this knowledge, why would I choose to comply, regardless of the consequences?

In response to my treatment in Case Study 2, I consciously crafted a work-life balance that prioritized my well-being and future success over investing additional efforts outside my job requirements into this organization, given its lack of respect and toxic work practices. I realized, I was the puzzle piece that did not fit and positioned myself to exit the company.

Support and Acceptance of the Group
(Case Study 2)

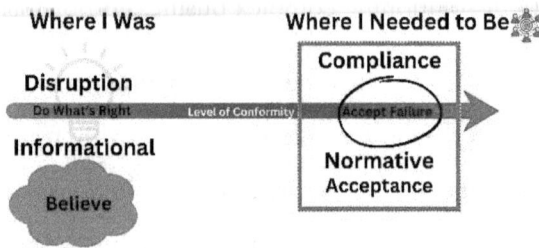

Disruptors are not merely anti-conformists; they question whether a decision or effort represents the best approach. Their motivation isn't to conform to fit into a group, avoid conflict, or gain acceptance but rather stems from a genuine belief that their approach or effort is the right one - so much so that they have internalized this information that is deeply ingrained in their identity, and the behavioral output is called Informational - Internalization. Disruptors have no desire to be a part of a group. They seek out like - minded individuals or communities that embody the same values. This is the distinct difference between a disruptor and a conformist. A disruptor's core values and beliefs are rooted in their actions. They're constantly assessing their environment and tasks for new opportunities for innovation. They engage with others who will challenge them. On the other hand, a conformist's core values and beliefs are often based on external factors and an internal desire to be a part of the group for personal gain or a feeling of safety - their desire to fit in drives their decision-making, resulting in groupthink and a lack of innovation.

True disruptive leaders are transformative and Agile. They not only welcome feedback, but they also seek it. It is in their DNA. It is built into their teams' ways of working. And when they engage with colleagues and superiors, this does not mean every suggestion is accepted, but every suggestion is genuinely considered. A Disruptive leader is not concerned with their subordinates outshining them or that their superiors will be threatened by their performance. If team members are not empowered to bring up crazy ideas, or they feel uncomfortable asking what may be perceived as a dumb question, you run the risk of missing some fantastic opportunities. Innovative approaches and ideas for improvement come from some of the most out-of-the-box ways of thinking. A team cannot function at this level and be innovative if its culture is based on social constructs that do not embrace open communication and a disruptive mindset.

Understandably, conformity is complex. It is driven by perceived social constructs, which can be categorized as informational or normative. Within this perception of social influence, a person conforms in one of three ways: compliance, identification, or internalization. As a leader, one challenge you will face is the range of team members on the spectrum of normative and informational, and you will need to either shift their mindset or meet them where they are to help drive the team towards success.

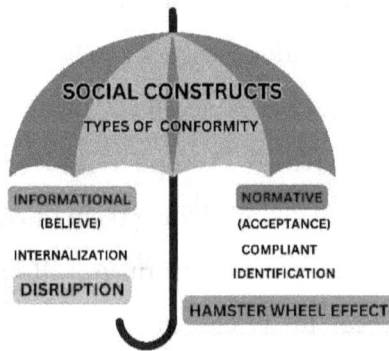

SOCIAL CONSTRUCTS
TYPES OF CONFORMITY

INFORMATIONAL (BELIEVE)
INTERNALIZATION
DISRUPTION

NORMATIVE (ACCEPTANCE)
COMPLIANT
IDENTIFICATION
HAMSTER WHEEL EFFECT

Normative Conformity is comprised of two categories: compliance and identification. The desire for group acceptance and avoidance of rejection drives it. This conformity is short-term and lacks a core belief foundation. When faced with a problem, individuals conform to group norms rather than seeking solutions. They may not challenge the group for fear of rejection, hindering sustainable change and innovation. Normative leaders perpetuate this cycle, often finding themselves trapped within it; they suffer from the **Hamster Wheel Effect**™.

Informational conformity stems from a core belief in the group's objectives rather than a desire to belong. Individuals in this category seek knowledge to advance the group's goals, demonstrating a long-term commitment to their beliefs. They make effective leaders as they prioritize understanding and value over mere agreement or pleasing others. Does this sound familiar? If connected to a group, a disruptive leader will gravitate to this type of conformity!

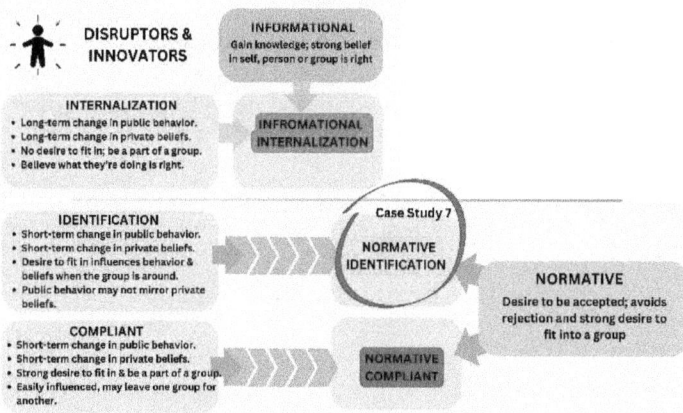

In Case Study 7 my leader stated, "I agree with you, but you can't or don't say that." This statement indicated my leader fell within the Normative - Identification category. Can you see the difference? My leader agreed with my approach, but the desire to fit within the group, avoid ostracism, or receive a consequence was a stronger motivator. In this instance, my leader chose to do what was easy over what was right. It is far easier to unfairly punish a subordinate and attempt to instill a basis of fear to ensure future compliance within the group than to speak up among your peers and senior leaders and say, "I don't agree with this approach."

If you commit to becoming someone committed to successful complex business problem solutioning, you need to believe what you are doing is right. You must have an unwavering belief like Elon Musk, as he was launching Tesla, that no matter what people say or do, it will not stop you from moving forward unless efforts do not add value.

HOW TO RECOGNIZE SOCIAL CONSTRUCTS

I.

As mentioned earlier, there is a concept in the field of change management called **Diffusion Innovation.** The idea is that cultural transformation does not occur overnight. Simply educating a population about the desired behaviors does not speed up cultural adoption. Simon Sinek of The Optimism Company notes that organizations make the biggest mistake by treating their cultural transformation as a marketing campaign. A cultural transformation is much more than a marketing campaign, it is a well-calculated strategy to ensure that not only is the transformation adopted, but it's also sustained and ultimately *ingrained* in your culture. Sound familiar to Information –Internalization?

Diffusion Innovation gives insight into how innovation is disseminated and catches on among a group of people. This diffusion can be in a small group, a large organization, an entire country, or even the world! It recognizes that not everyone will be supportive of the change initially. In fact, you will have more naysayers than supporters. The key is to believe that what you're doing is right. Your level of conformity must be at Informational-Internalization because you will need to weather the storm, especially if you are alone or not a part of a group that believes in change.

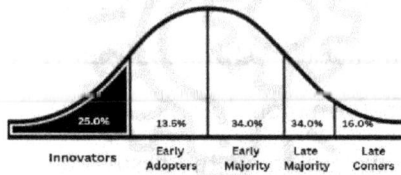

Cultural Transformation occurs over time, and if you are executing a transformation effort to solution a complex business problem, it is essential for you as a leader to recognize the various waves of Diffusion Innovation, the cadence of adoption, and the category of conformity people typically falls into:

Innovators lead change and believe wholeheartedly in the proposed change. They have internalized this belief, and their behavior demonstrates their position in both public and private. They speak with conviction about change and its importance. They are not talking or advocating to impress or gain acceptance; they share the knowledge they believe is right.

Early adopters believe in change. Although they are not present for the first wave of change, they will come in under the second wave and cause the necessary momentum or tipping point for the change to take effect. They tend to be leaders who have the ability to influence others and are typically viewed as the first to adopt and embrace change after an innovator. They either have internalized and believe in the change or the innovators themselves.

The Early Majority wholeheartedly supports the change. They delay adopting it because they take the time to research it before internalizing it. They may not be leaders, but once internalized, they become highly social and influential group members. They adopt because they have researched, believed in, and internalized the change.

The Late Majority recognizes that change is going to catch on and wants to be a part of it; they have not internalized the change. They either realize that the change is socially acceptable and adopt it or comply out of a desire to be a part of the group. They are usually change-resistant, but they may appear as if they are not because they are participating in the group.

Latecomers join after they see the large majority of people supporting the change go along with it as well because they are the last ones standing and desire to be a part of the group. They are highly change-resistant and do not believe in change.

The correlation between conformity and the various waves of diffusion innovation is intriguing. Conformity isn't static; it's dynamic, can evolve over time, and is influenced by exposure to new ideas and environments. Initially, individuals may seek acceptance and conformity to be a part of a group as they are exposed to the change. However, prolonged exposure can lead to a transition from seeking acceptance to becoming a believer in change. Conversely, individuals may initially believe in the change, even be the innovator that spearheaded the change. But over time, as their exposure continues and the change matures, they may begin to shift their level of conformity and eventually exit the group. This dynamic nature of conformity highlights its complex role in the diffusion of innovation, where individual's attitudes and behaviors can change as they interact with new ideas and experiences.

CASE STUDY 10

Core Values Trump Conformity

Garrett Camp, co-founder of Uber in 2009, and his partner Travis Kalanick launched the company to revolutionize communication and on-demand transportation. As innovators of the ride-sharing industry, the company gained a global platform through word-of-mouth and media coverage, appealing to early adopters seeking convenience in their transportation. Camp played a pivotal role in the company's early success. His belief in the service and vision for the company molded Uber's identity and culture, which resonated with employees, investors, and users. This fueled Uber's rapid growth and market dominance. Yet, with growth comes challenges, and as Uber began to face controversies like workplace harassment and ethical lapses, Camp passionately clashed with the company's direction. Pressure to conform to Uber's corporate culture conflicted with Camp's values of accountability and integrity. Despite his influential role, Camp chose to distance himself from Uber's operations, prioritizing principles over conformity.

In 2017, Garett decided to step away from the company's day-to-day operations. He demonstrated his genuine concern for the company's direction and, through an act of purposeful disruption, penned an exit letter that was transparent about the cause of his departure. He openly acknowledged the controversies surrounding the company and issued a call to action emphasizing the significance of accountability, integrity, and empathy in building a business. Garrett Camp is an innovator, disruptor, and leader who led with integrity. He resisted conforming to the group, emphasizing the significance of aligning personal core values with organizational goals, and was willing to sacrifice all that he achieved to maintain his integrity.

❀ ❀ ❀

II.

As you embark on a cultural transformation within your organization, you cannot expect everyone to adapt to the new culture immediately. Even after the culture has shifted, not everyone will internalize the transformation. Some may remain resistant, clinging to conflicting beliefs, potentially undermining progress, and attempting to sabotage your efforts. This dynamic is inherent in change and innovation within business operations. Change is never easy. Remember, over 78% of transformation efforts fail, but if you believe in what you are doing, transformation is possible!

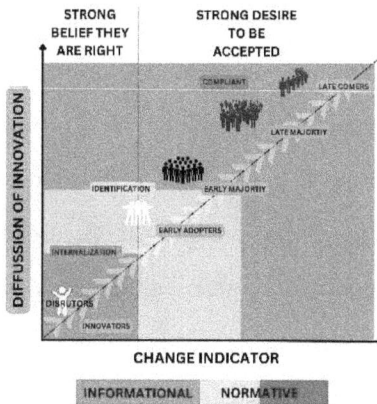

If you want to see Diffusion Innovation and Conformity in action, watch the YouTube video "Good Samaritan at Carnival Stop Out-of-Control Ride." In the video, a carnival ride full of passengers is quickly spinning, and you can see some of the bolts securing the ride to the ground have become dislodged. With each spin, the unbolted side rises higher and higher, and it is clear the ride is going to topple over. People watching were helplessly yelling for the operator to stop the ride, but clearly, it was too late, which at that point wouldn't have prevented the catastrophe. What do you think happened? One man (innovator) in the crowd runs towards the unbolted side and jumps on! He uses his weight to secure the unbolted side until the operator can stop the ride. Seeing his efforts, a few other people join him (early adopters). Eventually, others join in (early majority, late majority, and latecomers), ultimately providing enough weight to prevent the catastrophe.

The lesson here is that when you attempt to shift an organization's culture through transformation or solve a complex business problem, you likely will not initially get many people to support you. To succeed, you must lead with integrity and genuinely believe in what you are changing. I want to stress that transforming an organization's culture is neither easy nor finite. There are entire disciplines dedicated to these efforts. Several change management models are available to help you navigate cultural transformations, including Kotter's eight step model, Lewin's three-step change model, and the McKinsey & Company7-S model.

CASE STUDY 11

Non-Disruptive Conformist Leadership

A group of leaders across various departments and functions were aware of issues occurring within another department run by a colleague within their group. The colleague, a senior-level leader, oversaw a team whose poor performance not only impeded the progress of the various departments but also affected the organization. Water cooler conversations and internal complaints circulated, yet no group member spoke up to confront the problem directly.

This group observed excessive resource waste and unwarranted promotions within the senior-level leaders' team,

161

which all went unchallenged, possibly out of fear of political retaliation, an impact on their promotion, a culture rooted in conflict-avoidance, and an overall lack of leadership skills driven by a mindset and culture of 'good is good enough.'

Leaders participated in multiple meetings and openly complain about these issues and the impact on their departments and the organization. However, they never offered or attempted to identify solutions and rejected any proactive solutions any lower-level staff provided. This failure to address these issues head-on, which pervasively grew over the years, had a far-reaching impact on the organization and the employees. As you can imagine, the financial cost versus returns on investment caught the eye of the C-suite executives. They then asked the same group of senior-level leaders, who were aware of the problem but did not speak up, to resolve it.

After multiple half-hearted attempts to solution the problem, the C-suite executives stepped in. They decided to restructure the organization by waving their magic wand of power to solution what was believed to be the problem. This resulted in an entire department being dissolved. Multiple people lost their jobs, many of whom were highly skilled and added value to the organization. At no point was a complete problem solutioning analysis, feasibility, or impact assessment conducted. The assumption was that a few key employees, including the senior-level leader, were the issue. The unspoken solution was that by removing the entire group they would 'solve the problem.' As you can imagine, it did not. It only exposed more significant issues as time went on.

Albert Einstein said, *"We cannot solution our problems with the same level of thinking that created them."* Well, unfortunately, they didn't have Einstein as a consultant. They used the same thinking and approach, including failing to leverage industry best practices as a guide, and there were, of course, political grabs for power and recognition. It was heartbreaking to watch as my offers to help were rejected. As I stated before, I refused to play the political game, and unfortunately, politics over problem solutioning won.

It is a dangerous game to believe leadership should step in and wield a magic sledgehammer like Thor, the God of thunder who is called in to do a clean sweep and level the playing field, annihilate the problem, and save the day so everyone can start over! As a result, there is a sense of misguided urgency to meet senior executive leadership expectations and less urgency to take the time to understand the actual problems. There is an unspoken assumption that once the real problems have been resolved and the team causing them has been removed, now the focus can be on designing the new structure and establishing new processes. A good assessment should reveal the issues far deeper than what was felt by the department. Shockingly, what was believed to be the problem were symptoms of a larger problem within the organization. Recall the issues with the senior-level managers not voicing concerns; this is most likely a cultural and leadership development issue within the organization.

There is always quiet before the storm. If we've learned anything from superheroes, the villains, like problems, never return weaker. They come back stronger and present more significant challenges that require new skills, tools, and approaches to defeat them. After the department's dissolution, the organization had a series of mass layoffs to restructure. The same senior-level leadership who failed to speak up and address the blatant issues were the same individuals who had an opportunity for a do-over. While multiple highly competent and effective employees were let go.

❧ ❧ ❧

III.

Cultural Transformation and Disruptive Problem Solutioning™ are inherently interconnected; one cannot exist without the other. It would be ideal to have a major cultural transformation initiative simultaneously while you solution complex business problems. You may have to start small and gain momentum with one department or initiative at a time. I encourage you to be realistic and consider the culture, the leadership, your team's level of conformity, and what type of support you can secure before moving forward with solutioning. Keep in mind that what you think is the problem is more than likely a symptom of a larger problem. For instance, in case study 10, like the C-Suite, I initially believed that the senior-level leader and team were the problem. After removing the assumed problem, it was revealed that it was a complex symptom of a much more complicated problem within the organization, rooted in its culture, core values, and leadership capabilities. How can you easily solution this? The harsh reality is you can't.

When I see headlines that say a major corporation is pivoting to capitalize on the ever-changing market structure or restructuring to become leaner or more efficient, I genuinely want to know how many of those laid off are from within the core leadership team who more than likely failed to position the organization to be Agile and adapt its employees to a not so shockingly ever-changing market? The harsh reality is more than likely minimal, if any at all.

Operational problems are allowed to fester, and at the end of the year, a new approach is developed, and layoff season begins! Lower-level employees, managers, and directors lose their jobs or must hunt for new ones within an organization that has violated their trust and uprooted their stability. This is both frustrating and interesting because I have been on the receiving end of this behavior a few times. I am willing to bet those true leaders who are left unscathed have feelings of guilt, frustration, and powerlessness but don't know how to end the cycle.

One of the most interesting experiences I had during a layoff was the meeting with my direct supervisor and an HR representative. While being encouraged to apply for another position within the organization, I couldn't shake the feeling that my life was being drastically disrupted, yet it was nothing personal to them. Despite their pretense of genuine concern for my future, I couldn't help but question why the leadership responsible for the decision-making didn't take proactive measures during their strategic planning. Why wasn't there collaboration with HR to identify suitable positions aligned with my skills and offer a transition? It seemed like the burden was solely on me. I realized either no one cared enough to think innovatively to mitigate the impact of the layoffs, or it

Layoffs should never be the norm in any industry.

was deemed financially unviable to assist displaced employees in finding a new role internally. It appeared easier for them to enact layoffs, leaving the responsibility of figuring out the next steps solely on me. If there were a genuine concern, this approach wouldn't have been acceptable, but unfortunately, I knew it was far from genuine and it was all you could expect from a company that had to result in layoffs in the first place.

Through experience, I've learned that solely prioritizing an organization's needs can sometimes lead to unfulfilling outcomes. It's important to strike a balance and consider your well-being in the equation. Depending on your circumstances, weighing the potential consequences, and considering various paths forward may be beneficial: embracing change within the organization, finding ways to contribute while remaining true to your values, or exploring opportunities elsewhere.

These are difficult topics that are a harsh reality for many employees and leaders. As an employee, if your dollar value in your current role does not balance the income sheet, you no longer have value to the organization, and they will remove you. This addition underscores the importance of metacognition, open communication, and proactive steps toward positive change. By offering a solution-oriented approach with TAAP™, leaders are equipped with a tool to shift their mindset and effectively disrupt the status quo within their organization to ensure that as the company evolves and pivots to meet the demands of the market and technological advancements, its employees are simultaneously evolving and adapting as well. These employees retain their value as they continue to drive the company toward success.

PART THREE

Disrupt with Purpose

TACKLING COMPLEX BUSINESS PROBLEMS

I.

We've dedicated considerable time to discussing how to adapt your mindset and culture to address complex business problems and their repercussions. However, we have not delved into complex business problems and what they entail. Do you think you would know when you've encountered a complex business problem? If you answered, yes, then you are a problem-solutioning genius - think Einstein-Beethoven level! On the other hand, if you're uncertain don't worry; you're not alone in this journey. It's perfectly normal not to have all the answers right away.

I recall a valuable lesson from my Africana studies professor during my college years. He taught courses in advanced research and once shared something that profoundly affected me. He said, "I am not here to teach you anything. You've all gotten to this point because many have invested significant time teaching you things you were expected to know. I'm here, and you're in my class to learn that you don't, and will never, know everything - and it doesn't matter. What truly matters is that when faced with something you don't know, you have the skills and confidence to seek out the answer!"

Remember, every encounter is an opportunity for growth. On your journey towards growth, you don't need to have all the answers; you simply need skills and confidence to find them.

With any problem, you typically never know at first glance what level of complexity is hiding beneath the surface. You can only assume. However, encountering a problem with apparent symptoms and a seemingly quick fix doesn't mean you shouldn't attempt to address it. The faster you can solution a problem, or at minimum apply a band-aid, the less likely you are to impact the efficiency of your ecosystems. Be conscious of the fact that problems in business are rarely as simple as they appear.

II.

One of the most enlightening and impactful training courses I attended was a workshop on problem-solving. The facilitator split us into seven groups of five people, put up an image, and challenged us to solve it. He provided no context and gave us 20 minutes. He created a sense of urgency by saying that we would have no additional time and would be presenting our results to the group. People started immediately. There was this excitement in the air—*who would come up with the best solution?*

Here is the image. I challenge you to take a few minutes to find the problem and come up with a solution.

What did you come up with? What if I told you that there is no problem? No, this isn't a trick question. Did you answer from the bird's perspective that there is a problem because it is about to become the crocodile's next meal? Or did you reply from the perspective of the crocodile that there is no problem at all; this is a part of nature? Who are you to prevent a crocodile from having a delicious meal, right?

In a room full of Agile and Lean Six Sigma experts, the charts, graphs, theories, hypotheses, and metrics were abundant. We were all operating from a basis of assumptions about the relationship between the crocodile and the bird. The facilitator allowed each group to give a five-minute presentation on their problem statement and the proposed solution. When the presentations concluded, he asked, "Did anyone consider that there is no problem?" He pointed out that we spent almost an hour wasting time solutioning a problem that does not exist. The facilitator also pointed out that we all unquestioningly assumed there was a problem. Why did we do this? Was it because the facilitator said there was a problem to solve? Why didn't anyone ask probing questions before getting started? Why did we, as a collective group of supposed experts, not question others' assumptions and accept them as facts? Does this sound familiar? Do you recall the teacher-student, boss-subordinate dynamic we discussed earlier? What about conformity?

It seems we carry these behaviors with us into different settings, regardless of roles and professional expertise. In this example, the facilitator was seen as the boss, and it did not occur to anyone to question him. And if it did, no one spoke up. We trusted that he was the expert in the room and had the answers, and we were there to learn.

As you move towards a disruptive mindset, you must be conscious of your behaviors and habits because awareness is crucial in shifting your perspective. When faced with a problem, regardless of its origin, you must train your mind to ask questions at once. Is this the problem or a symptom of a more complex problem? Is this even a problem at all? You should have no fear or at least be able to overcome your fears and speak up. Remember, disruptors do not disrupt for the sake of disrupting. They disrupt to better understand the context of what they are doing to make informed decisions before they act. It is not easy being a disruptor, especially when you are part of a group that expects you to conform to unwritten and unspoken constructs rooted in the teacher-student dynamic.

Reflecting on the workshop, the facilitator convinced 35 professionals to not only adopt a tunneled visioned approach to solutioning a non-problem, but he had the entire group on a proverbial hamster wheel spinning as fast as we could with three simple words: solve this problem! As he watched in enjoyment and asked if anyone considered that there was no problem, we all went flying off the hamster wheel, confused, dazed, and back into reality. Pure genius!

Why was there no problem, you ask? We'll let me introduce you to the Egyptian Plover. It is a small bird known for its habit of entering the mouth of the crocodile, which, without context, would appear to be risky behavior. However, it is not as dangerous as it seems because the Egyptian Plover is agile and will likely be too swift for the crocodile to make a meal of it. The Egyptian Plover and the crocodile have a unique partnership referred to as "mutualistic symbiosis." The bird is nature's dental hygienist for crocodiles by providing cleaning services and picking parasites and food scraps from its teeth and gums. Recognizing the Egyptian Plover's benefit, the crocodile allows the bird to enter its mouth without harming it. The crocodile understands the benefits of the bird, so it would never eat it. These two incompatible species have developed a mutual understanding, so there is no problem.

There are many areas you will need to master to develop a disruptive mindset. In addition to facing your fears, you must avoid the trap of identifying the wrong problem and making assumptions, especially when tackling complex business problems. Don't be like the group of professionals in the workshop. We assumed the bird was in danger. We assumed there was a problem. In fact, one group assumed the problem was associated with global warming, resulting in the bird's unnatural behavior trying to find shelter from the heat!

Assumptions can lead to a waste of resources and time and misunderstandings. They can even lead us down a misguided path to find the solution. When tackling complex business problems, stay mindful of the peril that assumptions pose. Think of assumptions as concealed landmines in an open field. Initially, moving forward appears safe and harmless, but is it? You may have an unfounded sense of security and confidence, but by making these assumptions, you have clouded your vision and mistaken the feeling of safety as fact. With each successful step in a minefield, your confidence increases. However, the risk of making a mistake may also increase because a heightened level of confidence can lead to decreased caution.

Likewise, in problem-solutioning no matter how familiar you are with a problem, there are always unknown variables to consider. In truth, assumptions function as distractions that obscure your vision. When confronted with reality, assumptions detonate, leading to confusion and steering you further from the solution you've worked so hard to find.

Ultimately, assumptions often result in massive failures, leaving us dazed and confused, and few can recover from such setbacks.

CASE STUDY 12

An Assumption Took Down a Media Giant

Do you remember Blockbuster? Once dominating the movie rental industry, this worldwide rental chain - which employed tens of thousands of people across the United States, United Kingdom, Canada, Australia, Europe, and Asia - made the mistake of assuming that physical stores would always be the way people preferred to rent movies. They underestimated the shift in the market to a preference for digital technologies and online streaming services like Netflix. The assumption that their traditional model would remain dominant led to their filing for bankruptcy in 2010, and ultimately, their downfall. This media giant went from having thousands of stores to none.

Assumptions play a significant role in our daily lives, serving as mental shortcuts that help us navigate the complexities of the world. However, it's crucial to recognize when we're making assumptions and not confuse them with facts. Our brain naturally resorts to making assumptions due to several reasons. Firstly, cognitive efficiency is at play, where our brains aim to process information quickly to avoid cognitive overload. Secondly, our innate ability to recognize patterns and predict outcomes aids in making assumptions, contributing to our decision-making process. Social and cultural influences also shape our assumptions, aligning them with societal norms and values. Unfortunately, stereotypes can sometimes influence assumptions, leading to biases and unfair judgments. Heuristics, mental shortcuts, and confirmation bias further contribute to our tendency to make assumptions. By being mindful of these factors, we can make more informed decisions.

EMBRACE DISRUPTION

I.

Now that we have established the importance of a commitment to embrace TAAP™ to shift your mindset and the significance of organizational culture and transformation when solutioning complex business problems, let's delve into how we can be purposefully disruptive by leveraging **Disruptive Problem Solutioning™.** Through this approach, we'll explore how it can transform your organization's efforts to successfully solution complex problems. An added value-add is the development of a structured approach called B.E.S.T.™ that supports leaders embracing a Transformative Agile™ leadership style to operate more efficiently. Like Diffusion Innovation, Disruptive Problem Solutioning™ represents an approach aimed at not only solutioning problems but also seeking to initiate a cultural shift by disrupting traditional frameworks, methodologies, and mindsets regardless of the industry. To fully grasp the significance of Disruptive Problem Solutioning™ and its benefits, you must focus on executing holistic solutions.

In business, problems are persistent and will never cease to exist, whether simple or complex. Embracing this mindset shift will help you successfully position yourself and your organization to purposefully disrupt the status quo of your organization's current problem-solving approach. The goal is to cultivate an environment where complex business problems are gradually eliminated. This is achieved through leaders embracing TAAP™ and leveraging the Transformative Agile™ leadership style to create self-empowered and self-evolving teams. These teams are dedicated to both solutioning existing complex business problems and implementing sustainable solutions. Additionally, they proactively identify simple problems before they escalate into complex ones. The aim is to eradicate the existence of complex business problems, except in cases where they arise from unforeseen changes, such as advancements in the market, technology, or a product.

II.

A few years ago, I had a conversation with a colleague about the importance of individual skill levels in process improvement and its direct correlation to business problem solutioning. We quickly realized that when you first embark on addressing problems within an organization, your mindset is equally as significant as your skill level. When faced with a problem, if you find you don't have the skills to solution the problem, you have a few options. You can add skilled members to the team. You can learn the skills yourself. Also, in today's day and age, technological advancements allow you to use systems to fill skill gaps. Overall, if you lack the skills on your team, you have options to course correct.

If you kick off solutioning a problem with a limited mindset, your approach and level of success will be limited, too. For example, if your mindset is to simply 'solution the problem' because leadership said so, your focus is on resolving the problem. You may not be interested in understanding the origin of the problem or how to prevent it but simply want to make it go away to avoid the consequences of failing to meet leadership demands. If your criteria for success is based on leadership demands, this approach will work for you. However, this is a tunnel-vision approach rooted in the teacher-student dynamics. This is how people on hamster wheels solve problems.

We live in a society where competition is fierce regardless of industry. This approach aligns with a mindset of 'good is good enough.' Yes, there are situations where this approach may make sense to execute. Even if it makes sense, I wonder why you would ever want to be good enough when your competitors can usurp your standing in the market at any moment. Why not strive for excellence and position yourself to have a competitive edge?

Approaching a problem with the intent to solution it aligns with a commitment to achieve excellence because you are determined to go beyond simply fixing the issue. Solutioning a problem is a commitment to holistically viewing the problem from a strategic lens. Your goal is to develop a well-thought-out solution focusing on understanding how the problem occurred, how to prevent its reoccurrence or mitigate its impact, and how to support the implemented solution to ensure continued success.

A disruptive mindset is an agile mindset committed to driving the organization to consistently question conventional approaches by challenging existing norms. People with this mindset disrupt norms to ensure that the organization stays ahead of the curve as the industry evolves and new competitors enter the market. They are not driven by politics; they are driven by ideas! They ask questions, they address issues, and they are bold without fear of consequence. Disruptive Problem Solutioning™ is a commitment to excellence when solutioning complex business problems. I hope that you no longer solve business problems but you TAAP™ into your disruptive mindset and solution them.

II.

In addition to leaders having a disruptive mindset, employees should have one, too. What does this mean? As a leader, you need to be comfortable with not calling the shots. Your role is to establish the vision and provide resources.

You will need to:

1. Be humble and accept that you do not have all the answers.
2. Be comfortable with leading from the back of the room.
3. Provide the *what* and empower your staff to develop and execute the *how*.
4. In many ways, take on the characteristics of an Agile Scrum Master, removing impediments, such as political influence, pressure from senior leaders and others within the organization, and distractions that may prevent your team from focusing solely on solutioning the problem.
5. Be present for the team and take note of any support they may need, including:
   a. Providing support to team members who are struggling.
   b. Ensuring that your team stays motivated.
   c. Recognizing members' efforts as a collective.

d. Ensuring members possess the necessary skills for success by thinking ahead of the curve and providing resources for new skills to master as the industry and technology evolve.

Empowering your team to own *how* the problem will be solutioned and providing constructive feedback where appropriate can be done by not setting deadlines upfront. Deadlines should be driven by the amount of work required from resource-based feasibility and impact assessments completed by the team. To assign dates for the sake of what you want to deliver now is a guaranteed way to misguide a team whose focus should be on delivering excellence, not meeting unrealistic deadlines. I have found that often, leaders come up with unrealistic dates because they are either on a power trip, have failed to plan, or have a random idea that they have decided must get done right away after making assumptions about the requirements to complete the work. As leaders, I implore you to please stop.

III.

I will let you in on a little secret. Solutioning problems can be fun! Believe it. You can have fun with a dedicated team that has the right attitude, tools, and willingness to do the work. Think about it. Problems present exciting challenges. They require critical thinking and creativity, and there is even the opportunity to demonstrate your problem solutioning prowess. You must dig deep to identify the root cause of the issue, brainstorm innovative solutions, develop a plan, and then strategically implement your solution. Ultimately, the nail-biting moment begins when you monitor what you've put in place to see if you've identified the right solution or addressed a symptom of the problem. When problem solutioning is done right, you can unravel mysteries and overcome challenges with your teams' collective ingenuity. This can be intellectually stimulating, rewarding, and, yes, I said it, fun!

Furthermore, effective problem solutioning will lead to tangible and measurable outcomes, making it a gratifying experience. I have found that witnessing the positive impact of my problem-solutioning efforts encourages me to take on issues believed to be unsolvable. I live for the challenge of finding solutions to achieve the impossible. I learned early on that problem solutioning is not an individual endeavor. It requires a team, and I am always compelled to form an empowered team that can create positive change, overcome the most insurmountable obstacles, and contribute to the organization's growth, success, and bottom line. This gives me a great sense of accomplishment.

In my almost two decades of complex business problem-solutioning, I've observed good teams fail, including some of my own, regardless of the teams' level of dedication and commitment. If you're wondering why I didn't create my own original tool to solution complex business problems from scratch, you must first understand that I have spent decades committed to being efficient through innovation. Creating a tool from scratch would completely contradict my beliefs and values. Why would I reinvent the wheel when there are a plethora of proven tools, frameworks, approaches, and methodologies to solution complex problems readily available?

Far too often, we fail to use the resources available because we want to be recognized for something great. I understand how tempting this could be for some, but I am far less concerned with feeding my ego and more interested in creating approaches to strengthen a leader's ability to successfully solution complex business problems by leveraging the existing tools, frameworks, and methodologies to reduce the dismal failure rate of organizations who attempt to implement business transformations and change initiatives in an effort to solution complex business problems.

At this point, you've noticed I am placing a significant emphasis on the 'team' approach to solutioning complex business problems. When I first started on my solutioning journey, I tried to solution problems independently because I enjoy a sense of personal accomplishment. I initially found the opinions of others to be a distraction. I made decisions solely on instinct and first-hand knowledge. Over the years, I've learned that this approach was ineffective, and I would often solution a *symptom* of the problem instead of the problem itself. As I matured and explored various industries and approaches, I realized the power of a team who embraces Disruptive Problem Solutioning™. I encourage you to leverage the power of the team approach, no matter the urge to go at it alone.

If you are a leader or a leadership group who micromanages, Disruptive Problem Solutioning™ is not for you unless you are willing to change the way you work. Disruptive Problem Solutioning™ is based on two things: (1) Leaders who embrace TAAP™ and (2) a Transformative Agile™ leadership style comprised of self-evolving and self-empowered team members who are skilled with an ability to work collectively. They do not look to their leaders for permission to develop a plan and action solutions; they look to their leaders to provide a vision and a safe and solid foundation with sufficient resources to ensure they can focus on solutioning problems to achieve the defined vision.

Imagine a workplace where employees are not just cogs on the hamster wheel but are subject matter experts and professionals with unique skills and perspectives. You may say, "I already have this." My question(s) to you would then be, is your team self-evolving? Are they really empowered? Do they have autonomy? As a leader, how do you view them? Do you provide tasks and assignments for them to complete? Do you oversee and approve their work? Do you respect them because they bring something valuable to the table, possibly a skill or experience you may not have? Are you threatened or intimidated by lower-ranking employees with advanced skills? Do you operate from a basis of fear? Fear they may outshine you, fear they may know the answer to something you don't, or fear they don't need you?

Assess how you have behaved towards empowered employees in the past. Have you avoided them? Or decided not to hire someone who is self-empowered because you felt they were overqualified or more qualified than you? Leaders who operate from a basis of fear typically make fear-based decisions and micromanage. In this world of modern business, where markets are ever-changing, we will face a paradigm shift where forward-thinking organizations will recognize that the traditional top-down, hierarchical micromanagement-driven approach is no longer practical; in fact, it is detrimental to the health and survival of an organization.

IV.

We always hope for an easy fix—a simple change that will erase a problem with the stroke of a pen or a stern word from someone in authority. Rarely does anything in life work this way. And when it does, it is usually a Band-Aid, a temporary fix that will eventually start to peel away at the seams and give way to a bigger problem that has festered for far too long.

I am not suggesting that we not take advantage of quick fixes; in Disruptive Problem Solutioning™, quick fixes are welcomed, but you should be clear that they are not the solution. They are temporary Band-Aids to gain some leverage over an escalating situation while the team works to solution the problem. This is where selecting the right approach and knowing which tools to use comes into play.

Evolution of Problem Solutioning

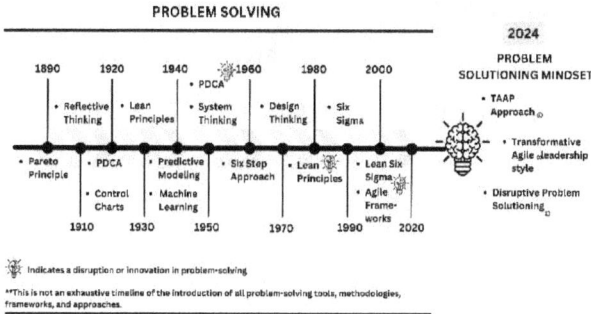

PROBLEM SOLVING

2024

PROBLEM SOLUTIONING MINDSET

1890	1920	1940	1960	1980	2000

- PDCA

- Reflective Thinking
- Lean Principles
- System Thinking
- Design Thinking
- Six Sigma

- TAAP Approach
- Transformative Agile Leadership style
- Disruptive Problem Solutioning

- Pareto Principle
- PDCA
- Predictive Modeling
- Six Step Approach
- Lean Principles
- Lean Six Sigma
- Agile Frameworks

- Control Charts
- Machine Learning

1910	1930	1950	1970	1990	2020

Indicates a disruption or innovation in problem-solving

**This is not an exhaustive timeline of the introduction of all problem-solving tools, methodologies, frameworks, and approaches.

Despite the significant advancements in technology and the expansion of global industries, the last significant introduction of a problem-solving methodology` occurred over 20 years ago. This gap has left organizations struggling to adapt to the new complexities presented by modern business challenges. No wonder a staggering 78% of major initiatives aimed at solutioning complex business problems end in failure. It's clear that relying solely on a traditional five or seven-step approach is no longer effective in addressing the multifaceted issues businesses face today. I am not suggesting that the tools themselves are connected to the failure rate of initiatives; as a certified Lean Six Sigma Black Belt, I thoroughly understand the value problem-solving tools provide. While these tools remain invaluable, we need to continue to delve into the root cause of why initiatives and transformations are failing. If it is not the tools, what is it?

The core values of Disruptive Problem Solutioning™ are based on the 3Cs of Agile: Collaboration, Coordination, and Communication. Teams are structured to function harmoniously in an environment where they efficiently work together without fear or micromanagement, an environment where they can embrace change, deliver valuable outcomes, and actively foster a team culture rooted in a commitment to adaptability, continuous improvement, and sustainability.

If you are like most people who have worked on teams struggling to solution problems, it must sound like I am trying to sell you snake oil. I promise you I am not. Efficient, effective, and consistently successful problem solutioning teams can exist! Disruptive Problem Solutioning™ is all about bringing your A-game when assembling your team to successfully solution complex business problems.

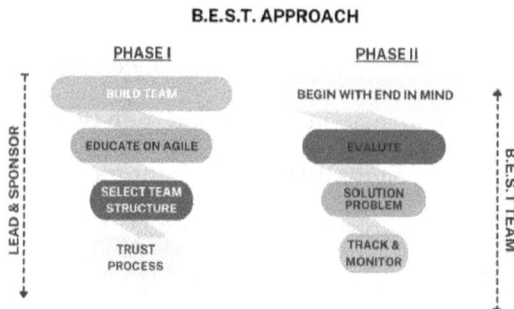

B.E.S.T. APPROACH

PHASE I	PHASE II
BUILD TEAM	BEGIN WITH END IN MIND
EDUCATE ON AGILE	EVALUTE
SELECT TEAM STRUCTURE	SOLUTION PROBLEM
TRUST PROCESS	TRACK & MONITOR

LEAD & SPONSOR

B.E.S.T TEAM

The acronym B.E.S.T.™ guides this approach:

Phase I: Build Your Team

B: Build the Team

Gather a diverse group of individuals with complementary skills and perspectives. The key here is that team members include participants from various levels within the organization.

E: Educate on Agile

Ensure team members understand agile principles and methodologies to foster collaboration and adaptability.

S: Set Team Structure

Establish clear roles, responsibilities, and communication channels to streamline collaboration and decision-making.

T: Trust the Agile Process

Encourage trust in the agile process, promoting transparency, experimentation, and continuous improvement.

Phase II: When the Team is Formed

B: Begin with the End in Mind

Define the symptoms, problems, and desired future state or outcome clearly to guide the team's efforts. Identify the tools, methodologies, approaches, and frameworks you will leverage to solution the problem.

E: Evaluate the Symptoms

Measure and analyze the underlying issues or challenges through a systematic evaluation process. Validate that you have identified the problems and not a solution masking the problem.

S: Solution the Problem

Develop and implement targeted improvements or solutions to address the identified issues effectively.

T: Track and Monitor Progress

Establish mechanisms to track progress, measure outcomes, and maintain oversight to ensure alignment with goals, objectives, and sustainability.

If you would like to delve deeper into B.E.S.T.™ and unlock its full potential, stay tuned for upcoming resources where I'll provide comprehensive guidance and detailed insights. Keep an eye out for additional information that will take your complex problem solutioning skills to the next level! You can visit www.idapmack.com for updates!

V.

As early as the 1800s, although they were not formalized, there were problem-solving methodologies that laid the groundwork for the evolution of problem-solving in the 20th century. The Pareto Principle was the first problem-solving tool and was introduced 127 years ago in 1896. Also known as the 80/20 rule, Vilfredo Pareto noted that 80% of the land in Italy was owned by 20% of the population. Today, this principle is widely used to prioritize efforts or resources and to focus on the most impacted areas. If you recall, in Chapter 3, I said leadership development is 80% self-development and 20% education. Well, this reflects the Pareto Principal!

One of the first tools of the 20th century was called reflective thinking, also known as critical thinking or introspection. It emerged as a significant concept in 1910 and involves the thoughtful analysis of one's thoughts, experiences, and actions to gain a deeper understanding. *Have you noticed that I've integrated reflective thinking by encouraging you to be introspective throughout the book?*

In the 1920s and 1930s, interest in problem-solving began to pick up. Walter Shewhart introduced a tool called the Plan-Do-Check Act (PDCA), which was made popular in the 1950s by W. Edwards Demming. It's also referred to as the Demming Cycle, which is one of the first systematic approaches to solution simple and complex problems. Around the same time, in 1924, the control chart, which laid the foundation for modern quality control methods, was introduced. By the 1930s, there was garnered interest in problem-solving with the introduction of Lean principles and practices which focused on minimizing waste and maximizing efficiency. This approach was the first major disruption to problem-solving when it was popularized in the 1980s through a publication called "The Machine that Changed the World." Over the next 40 years, more than ten tools and techniques were introduced, and most are commonly used today.

As problem-solving became more popular, Six Sigma emerged on the scene in 1986, thanks to Motorola. It proved to be disruptive to the field when General Electric popularized it in the 1990s. The introduction of Six Sigma was unique because it brought about a systematic approach to reducing defects and variations in processes. By prioritizing data-driven decision-making, process enhancement, and customer satisfaction, Six Sigma led to notable advancements in quality and efficiency across various industries.

Lean and Six Sigma merged in the latter part of the 20th century, primarily during the 1990s and early 2000s. This merger stemmed from the acknowledgment that both methodologies provide complementary strategies for enhancing processes and managing quality. By blending Lean's principles for minimizing waste with Six Sigma's methods for reducing defects, companies amplified their enhancements in efficiency, quality, and customer satisfaction.

Since its introduction in the early 2000s, Agile frameworks—which originally were developed for software— have found a home in various industries because of their flexibility and adaptability to collective problem-solving approaches; other advancements have emerged in the realm of modern problem-solving to address the evolving needs of organizations. These advancements include Advanced Data Analytics (e.g., predictive modeling, machine learning, artificial intelligence (AI) technologies) and Design Thinking, which is a human-centered approach to solutioning complex business problems focusing on innovation and problem-solving. Similar to Agile frameworks, it emphasizes the needs of the user through developing creative solutions and rapidly prototyping and testing ideas. And like Agile, its core focus is encouraging iterative development within the team.

Despite the emergence of groundbreaking advancements in problem-solving tools, frameworks, and approaches such as Agile frameworks, Advanced Data Analytics, and Design Thinking, the success rate of organizations solutioning complex business problems through change initiatives and business transformations continues to decline. This begs the question again: why are failure rates so high despite the abundance of tools, systems, and availability of skilled subject matter experts? The answer lies in recognizing that successful complex business problem solutioning begins well before selecting a team, a tool, or a framework or methodology. It begins with the mindset of the leader.

No matter how advanced or effective a tool may be, its impact is only as good as the mindset of the leader guiding the team implementing it.

Consider a skilled carpenter with access to the finest tools but lacking the vision, integrity, and courage to challenge traditional methods of craftsmanship. Each flaw in their mindset is mirrored in their actions, which diminishes the likelihood of not only selecting the right tools but also utilizing them to deliver quality products while exploring more efficient crafting techniques. Now, what if the carpenter had a team of skilled craftsmen who brought diverse experiences and perspectives to the table? Even with the best tools at their disposal, the team's success is contingent upon the carpenter's ability to guide them to deliver the vision.

Similarly, when solutioning complex business problems, the leader's mindset is paramount in guiding a team towards a solution. The leader's mindset is demonstrated in the behaviors they exhibit through their leadership style, communication style, agility, ethics, core values, and readiness to challenge the status quo - all crucial factors in successful complex business problem solutioning. In reality, with every gap or weakness in the leader's mindset, the journey to solutioning complex business problems becomes more arduous, and success is less likely for the entire team.

While new approaches have proven valuable, there remains a critical gap in addressing the mindset of leaders. It is time to disrupt our approach and shift our focus. Instead of starting with the selection of tools, we must begin to change the norm for our leaders. Knowingly, leaders who embrace TAAP™ hold themselves accountable. They lead self-empowered teams who embrace Disruptive Problem Solutioning™ with a focus on not only solutioning complex business problems but preventing them from developing in the first place.

VI.

When you began this journey, key areas were identified to shift your mindset from an assigned to a self-accountable leader who understands the gravity of your decisions. You should have a clear understanding of the theoretical application of the various leadership styles and the benefits of a being a Transformative Agile™ leader with the power to forge self-empowered and self-evolving teams to sustain the solution that has been put in place. You've delved into the essence of ethical leadership - the significance of leading with integrity and aligning your core values with your organizations. You've explored the dynamics of the teacher-student and boss-

198

subordinate mindset, recognizing the need to liberate yourself and your team from fear-based decision-making. Most importantly, you've uncovered the power of 'Self' and gained insight into the importance of social constructs and conformity. It is through the power of 'Self' that you can drive innovation and be purposeful in disruption. You can lead and transform teams that successfully solution complex business problems.

It's time to challenge industry standards and reject norms rooted in a 'good is good enough' mindset. Here's your roadmap:

1. Embrace TAAP™ and evolve into a Transformative Agile™ leader.
2. Forge B.E.S.T.™ teams dedicated to Disruptive Problem Solutioning™.
3. Through the power of 'Self,' commit to an ongoing leadership journey.

Remember, it is not the distance traveled, but the experiences gained that fuel growth. Empower yourself to disrupt with purpose and drive change. Your organization's success depends on it!

ACKNOWLEDGEMENTS

Thank you to my family, friends, and colleagues who encouraged me to dream big and supported me during the creation of Escaping the Hamster Wheel.

I want to give special thanks to my editor, Nailah Harvey, for challenging me to create an approach that can benefit readers beyond the book.

I also want to express my gratitude to Jasmine Womack (From Paid to Published) and Ashley Kirkwood (Speak Your Way to Cash). Your wealth of resources and expertise gave me the confidence to publish Escaping the Hamster Wheel and create valuable services for my clients through LuminEssence Consulting Group.

RESOURCES

Escaping the Hamster Wheel

To access information on any of the resources below, go to www.idapmack.com

FREE RESOURCES

Escape the Hamster Wheel™ Facebook Group

A Facebook group with content aimed at providing resources to support leaders on their leadership development journey. Content is focused on the key topics covered in Escaping the Hamster Wheel and its companion workbook. It is perfect for leaders who are thinking about or have begun their journey of self-empowerment and self-accountability. This is not a problem solutioning community but rather a member-led, free Facebook community.

Disruptive Problem Solutioning™ Institute Toolbox

This toolbox provides resources, including problem-solving tools, articles, and videos to help you use the proper tools, frameworks, methodologies, and approaches on your solutioning journey.

Escape the Hamster Wheel™ Employee Coaching

This is a free service limited to 12 employees a year who have experienced a layoff. There are two structured programs a year (September-November) and (May-July) dedicated to completing the Escaping the Hamster Wheel book and companion workbook. These group sessions are not related to assisting with employment; they are modeled after the Escaping the Hamster Wheel book and workbook. The program includes 6 group sessions, including pre-work, which is assigned prior to each session. There is also a private Facebook group to provide additional support during participation in the program.

PAID OFFERINGS

Escape the Hamster Wheel™ Workshop

This is an intensive 5-day workshop dedicated to supporting leaders, groups, and companies to develop a custom roadmap to Escape the Hamster Wheel and Disrupt with Purpose!

Disruptive Problem Solutioning™ Workshop

This is an intensive seven-day workshop designed to equip leaders with the skills, tools, and mindset to tackle complex business problems head-on and solution them effectively!

Agile Workshop Development

Ida and her team will work with you to create a fun and engaging workshop rooted in Agile principles and training from the back of the room approaches to ensure you achieve the desired outcomes and participants benefit from attendance.

ONE-ON-ONE SERVICES

Disruptive Problem Solutioning™ Strategy Session

Three intensive 2-hour sessions with Ida to help you develop a roadmap to plan a strategy to solution a complex business problem. This session is an excellent opportunity to gain clarity and perspective to ensure you, as a leader, have the best strategy in place to kick off your solutioning journey.

Escape the Hamster Wheel™ Leadership Agile Coaching

A 6-month intensive Agile leadership coaching program with Ida, a certified Agile Coach, to support leaders on their self-empowerment and self-accountability journey to disrupt with purpose. This is an exclusive service limited to 6 leaders a year.

EVENT OFFERINGS

Escape the Hamster™ Wheel Live Event!

Designed for those who have a conference, interactive town hall, offsite, corporate event, or any gathering for entrepreneurs or leaders. This interactive event features a Keynote speech from Ida and a series of customized metacognitive workshops designed to jump-start participants' paths to disrupt with purpose! Ten percent of proceeds from all Live Events are donated to assist those who are at risk of or have been unhoused due to being laid off.

NOTES

Chapter 1

1. Anderson, E. (2021, September 27). Beating the odds-on organizational change. *Forbes*. Retrieved from https://www.forbes.com/sites/erikaandersen/2021/09/27/beating-the-odds-on-organizational-change/?sh=1773fde1cf54

2. Senge, P. (2006). *The fifth discipline: The art & practice of the learning organization*.

3. Kotter, J. P. (2012). *Leading change*.

4. Shenab, H. (2018). The science behind approach, methodology & framework: Are they really different? [LinkedIn article]. Retrieved from https://www.linkedin.com/pulse/science-behind-approach-methodology-framework-really-different-hatem/

5. Axelrod, T. (2001). *Hans and Sophie Scholl: German resistors of the White Rose*.

6. Bazigos, M. (2016). Revisiting the matrix organization. *McKinsey & Company*. Retrieved from https://www.mckinsey.com/capabilities/people-and-organizational-performance/our-insights/revisiting-the-matrix-organization

7. Ratanjee, V., & Dvorak, N. (2018). Mastering matrix management in the age of agility. *Gallup*. Retrieved from https://www.gallup.com/workplace/242192/mastering-matrix-management-age-

agility.aspx#:~:text=Gallup%20analytics%20finds%2084%25%20of%20U.S.%20employees%20are,day%2C%20reporting%20to%20the%20same%20or%20different%20managers.

8. Roddick, A. (2001). *Business as unusual*.

9. Litwin, L. (2002). *Fannie Lou Hamer: Fighting for the right to vote*.

10. Mandela, N. (1995). *A long walk to freedom*.

11. Bradberry, T. (2009). *Emotional EQ 2.0*.

12. Inside Amazon: Wrestling big ideas in a bruising workplace. (2015). *The New York Times*. Retrieved from https://www.nytimes.com/2015/08/16/technology/inside-amazon-wrestling-big-ideas-in-a-bruising-workplace.html

Chapter 2

13. Murphy, M. (2019). *Leadership styles*.

14. Drucker, P. (2008). *Management*.

15. The Enneagram Institute. (n.d.). *The Enneagram Institute*. Retrieved from https://www.enneagraminstitute.com

Chapter 3

16. Deming, E. (2012). *The essential Deming: Leadership principles from the father of quality*.

17. Killeen, F. (2020). What the hell is a digital transformation, and why is it failing 78% of the time?

[LinkedIn article]. Retrieved from
https://www.linkedin.com/pulse/what-hell-digital-transformation-why-failing-78-time-finn-killeen/

18. McKinsey & Company. (2021). *Losing from day one: Why even successful transformations fall short* [PDF]. Retrieved from
https://www.mckinsey.com/~/media/mckinsey/business%20functions/people%20and%20organizational%20performance/our%20insights/successful%20transformations/december%202021%20losing%20from%20day%20one/losing-from-day-one-why-even-successful-transformations-fall-short-vf.pdf

Chapter 4

19. Christensen, C. (2017). *The innovator's dilemma: When new technologies cause great firms to fail*.

20. Mann, J., & Kay, G. (2024). Read the memo Elon Musk sent Tesla staff announcing that the company is laying off more than 10% of the workforce. *MSN*. Retrieved from
https://www.msn.com/en-us/money/companies/read-the-memo-elon-musk-sent-tesla-staff-announcing-that-the-company-is-laying-off-more-than-10-of-the-workforce/ar-BB1lEcjE

21. Hsieh, T. (2010). How Zappos infuses culture using core values. *Harvard Business Review*. Retrieved from
https://hbr.org/2010/05/how-zappos-infuses-culture-using-core-values

22. Black, S. (2023). Massive layoffs are coming. *Newsweek*. Retrieved from https://www.newsweek.com/mass-layoffs-happening-2024-hiring-freeze-1855942

23. McCarthy, J. (2017). A lifetime of planting trees on a remote river island: Meet India's Forest Man. *NPR*. Retrieved from https://www.npr.org/sections/parallels/2017/12/26/57242159 0/hed-take-his-own-life-before-killing-a-tree-meet-india-s-forest-man

Chapter 6

24. Bainbridge, C. (2023). What is a social construct? Why every part of society is a social construct *Very well mind*. Retrieved from https://www.verywellmind.com/definition-of-social-construct-1448922#History%20of%20Social%20Constructionism

25. Rogers, E. M. (2003). *Diffusion of innovations*.

Chapter 8

26. Davis, T., & Higgins, J. (n.d.). A blockbuster failure: How an outdated business model destroyed a giant. Retrieved from https://ir.law.utk.edu/cgi/viewcontent.cgi?article=1010&contex t=utk_studlawbankruptcy

Chapter 9

27. Womack, J. P., Jones, D. T., & Roos, D. (2017). *The machine that changed the world: The story of lean production – Toyota's secret weapon in the global car wars that is now revolutionizing the industry*.

28. The Deming Institute. (n.d.). *Deming 101: Understanding systems*. Retrieved from https://deming.org/deming-101-understanding-systems/

Ida Mack is the founder and Managing Director of LuminEssence Consulting Group, a boutique agency specializing in leadership development and providing solutions for complex business challenges. With expertise as a Lean Six Sigma Black Belt, certified Agile Coach, and Agile Workshop Facilitator, Ida has dedicated over two decades to problem-solutioning. Her experience culminates in the authorship of *Escaping the Hamster Wheel: A Disruptive Approach to Solutioning Complex Business Problems* and its companion workbook.